LIGHT FOR LIFE

Part Two

The Mystery

Celebrated

God With Us Publications

Catechesis is a work of the Church, a sharing in the teaching mission of the Body of Christ. Catechetical material, like iconography or liturgical chant, strives to speak of the Tradition of the Church. The individual's insights, perceptions, and experiences become significant in that they personalize this Tradition and give witness to it in our contemporary world.

Accordingly, each text is the work of those Byzantine Catholic Churches in North America which participate in ECDD, the catechetical arm of the bishops of Eastern Catholic Associates. Contributors to this text include Father David Petras, principal contributor, with Father Fred Saato and Deacon Kent Plowman of the Ruthenian and Melkite Greek Catholic jurisdictions respectively. The text was subsequently reviewed and approved by all the hierarchs of the thirteen participating dioceses, their directors of religious education and diocesan catechetical staffs. It therefore represents their communities' common faith and vision.

Iconographic drawings: Rev. Mark Melone
Cover design: Beverly Stoller, Studio of the Theotokos

GOD WITH US PUBLICATIONS
P.O. Box 99203
Pittsburgh, PA 15233

Printed in the U.S.A.

ISBN 1-887158-09-X (Part Two)
!SBN 1-887158-06-5 (Three Part Set)
Library of Congress Catalogue Card Number 96-077418

Table of Contents

Acknowledgements

The versions of Scripture traditionally used in Byzantine Churches have been the Septuagint version of the Old Testament (LXX) and the "received text" of the New Testament. Whenever necessary, these readings have been translated for this work. Otherwise, sources for Scriptural citations are:

JB — *The Jerusalem Bible*, copyright 1966, Darton, Longman & Todd, Ltd.
NAB — *The New American Bible*, copyright 1970, the Confraternity of Christian Doctrine
RSV — *The Revised Standard Version,* copyright 1971, Division of Christian Education, National Council of Churches of Christ
TEV — *Today's English Version*, copyright 1966, American Bible Society

When references to the LXX and the Hebrew text differ, as in the numbering of the psalms, the LXX citation is given first.

Whenever possible, liturgical texts have been cited from versions in use among the Byzantine Catholic jurisdictions in North America.

About the Cover - In the Byzantine tradition, the highpoint of THE MYSTERY CELEBRATED is the Divine Liturgy, the actualization of the presence of Christ where two or three are gathered in His name. The icon of the Liturgy depicted here illustrates two characteristics which the Byzantine tradition ascribes to the Liturgy. Its continuity with the apostolic tradition is suggested in the persons of the celebrants, St James the Bishop of Jerusalem and the protomartyr, the deacon St Stephen. Its connection with the heavenly liturgy is indicated by the ripidion, symbol of the presence of the angels, with which the deacon fans the Holy Gifts.

1 — Faith Expressed in Worship

Life is a mystery. Elements of it are partially understandable, but these do not exhaust its possibilities. Central to seeing life in its fullness is faith in a loving Creator who reveals His presence to us as *our* "way, truth and life" (Jn 14:6). This faith—ultimately a gift of God—is an invitation to rediscover our world in the light of God and to celebrate His loving-kindness in worship.

The Church's tradition of worship profoundly reflects the depth and breadth of the reality of God's love for us and His mystical union with us. We can hear the still, small voice of God[1] speaking to our inner being across the ages with His timeless voice of love, and come to recognize it when we hear it in other ways.

Worship is a "bowing down" (Greek, *proskynesis*) or an "act of service" (Greek, *latreia*); but in this very act of emptying ourselves before God, we are filled with His Spirit and made God-like. Worship is glorification (Greek, *doxologia*) of the Other: our Creator, Savior and Lifegiver; but this act of glorifying the Other lifts us as creatures to the pinnacle of human expression. Our smallness in a vast universe may seem to reduce us to insignificance. However, the act of giving glory to God by our own free will opens to us the true greatness of our destiny unmatched in all of inanimate creation. It is only when we render the glory, honor and worship due to God that we discover the true dignity of our human calling: to participate in the life and love of the Creator.

Worship should not be mistaken as arbitrary servitude to a jealous God. This wrong concept masks the true meaning of worship: a simple awareness of our true relationship with God. The word itself implies "worth-ship" or the giving of honor where it is truly due.

Worship recognizes our complete need for God; and recognizing this dependence elevates us into His very life.

Christians further understand worship in the light of Christ and our union in Him. Having put on Christ in baptism, we have been brought into the mystery of Jesus Christ and empowered to join ourselves to the perfect worship which Christ continually offers to the Father. In the Church's worship we participate in Christ's work of salvation through the Holy Spirit, who prays for us in a way which transcends human language (Rom 8:26). Thus it is not we who initiate worship; rather we cooperate with Christ while He transforms and deifies us.

WORSHIP AS SACRIFICE

Worship is an act which signifies both our complete openness to God and our desire for union with Him. It is an offering of self — a sacrifice — expressed in words, in gestures, in deeds. This attitude is expressed in the so-called Standard Beginning or Trisagion Prayers, with which most Byzantine liturgical services open[2]. This sequence, culminating in the Lord's Prayer which proclaims our dedication to the kingdom of God, express the worshipper's self-offering in word (the prayers) and gestures (the metanies, the sign of the cross). These prayers, like any sacrifice, reflect the spirit of openness to God which marks the believer as distinct from those who do not believe.

In the Old Testament era the spirit of sacrifice was expressed in the temple sacrifices of animals or food. Making these offerings expressed the worshipper's desire for union with God, but they could not achieve it. This unity could only be accomplished in Christ:

Since the Law has only a shadow of the good things to come and not the true form of these realities, it can never perfect the worshippers by the same sacrifices offered continually year after year. ... but Jesus offered one sacrifice for sins and took His place forever at the right hand of God. ... by one offering He has forever perfected those who are being sanctified (Heb 10:1,12,14).

NOH OFFERS SACRIFICE

"Then Noah built an altar to the Lord, and took of every clean animal and of every clean bird, and offered burnt offerings on the altar" (Gn 8:20).

7

Christ did not offer a gesture or token sacrifice, but the complete and total sacrifice of His entire being. Through this unique sacrifice, made present to us in the Divine Liturgy, we are "perfected": truly united with God, totally transformed and made holy. Because of this union, Christian worship is an entirely new reality, what St. Paul called *spiritual worship*[3]: "I beg you, through the mercy of God, to offer your bodies as a living sacrifice holy and acceptable to God, your spiritual worship" (Rom 12:1).

EARTHLY PARTICIPATION IN HEAVENLY LIFE

The commentaries of the Fathers often draw comparisons between the earthly liturgy and the heavenly liturgy. This resemblance is inspired by the prophecy of Isaiah, who had a vision of angels surrounding God's throne singing, "Holy, holy, holy is the Lord of Hosts! All the earth is filled with His glory!" (6:3). In the New Testament, the Book of Revelation depicts God seated in the midst of angels and the twenty-four elders who sing, "To the One seated on the throne and to the Lamb be blessing and honor and glory and power forever and ever." (Rev 5:13)

This theme of heavenly worship recurs frequently in Byzantine liturgical services with their frequent mention of the angelic hosts:

> The cherubim who stand with fear in Your presence and the seraphim who quake and tremble offer to You with ceaseless voices the thrice-holy hymn. Together with them we sinners cry out: "Holy, holy, holy are You, O God! Through the prayer of Your saints, have mercy on us."

(Troparion for Lenten Matins, Sixth Tone)

At the Divine Liturgy, after the holy gifts are sanctified, we pray that they may be received "on [God's] holy, heavenly, and mystical altar." "Standing at this holy altar as before Your cherubic throne" (Presanctified Liturgy), we offer to God a worship which has a spiritual

8

reality that goes beyond what we see on the surface. The person who does not see with the eyes of faith, perceives worship as mere words and ritual gestures. Those illuminated by faith see it as "God with us" sanctifying us and, through us, the world in which we live.

WORSHIP AND THE CONTINUING SALVATION OF THE WORLD

The Church's worship celebrates the eternal truth that God is in our midst, working for our salvation. He has inclined the heavens by the incarnation of Christ and brought us into the life of heaven in the resurrection. Liturgy expresses this life in Christ flowing from our union with God and nourishing us as His children. Christ said, "I am the vine, you are the branches. He who lives in me and I in him, will produce abundantly, for apart from me you can do nothing" (Jn 15:5). Liturgical worship has been described as living in heaven-on-earth, because it is there that we are nourished by the vine which is Christ.

As the Lord said, he who is so nourished is meant to produce abundantly. And so our liturgical life calls us to a mission which extends beyond the sanctuary. The Church's worship extends our individual profession of faith to include a commitment to God's plan of salvation for the whole world. The services themselves express this commitment through intercession for "peace throughout the world, the welfare of the holy Churches of God and the union of all" (Great Litany), drawing all persons and nations into our worship. Our involvement in worship also calls us to focus our attention on works of concern for those for whom we pray. "Our Father, who art in heaven... Thy Kingdom come," would be a vain prayer without it.

WORSHIP AS A NORM OF FAITH

Our action of worship is more than a token of faith; it is our faith itself in action. This is why the Fathers insisted so often that our worship constitutes our belief and why formulas of faith ("word symbols") are drawn from our liturgical life. St. Irenaeus taught this as early as the second century, "Our teaching is in accordance with the Eucharist, and the Eucharist in turn establishes our teaching."[4]

As an element of the Tradition, the work of the Holy Spirit in the Church, liturgical worship is a norm of faith, a source and pattern for life. We are not free to alter it arbitrarily, to treat it as mere entertainment or to reject it as irrelevant without separating ourselves from faith. We live in a society which tempts us to do so because it is both individualistic and subjective. Rather than draw faith from our worship, we have a tendency to force faith to conform to our preconceptions. Instead of seeking a source and pattern for life in our worship, we may try to find refuge from our personal cares and problems.

LITURGY IS A COMMUNAL REALITY

Liturgy is meant for celebration within a community. It is not merely a setting for private prayer or meant as a supplement to our individual spiritual life. Christian worship is based on the New Testament revelation of God as a "community" of Father, Son and Holy Spirit. When we are baptized into Christ we are made children of the Father and bearers of the Spirit, truly members by extension of the community of the Trinity. Together with all the baptized we are being joined together as a holy temple, "built together spiritually into a dwelling place for God" (Eph 2:22). We are enjoined to let ourselves be the living stones of this temple: "Let yourselves be built into a spiritual house, to be a holy priesthood, to offer spiritual sacrifices acceptable to God through Jesus Christ" (1 Pt 2:5).

The Church's worship is precisely God's instrument for making us a people, forming us into His kingdom—"The Kingdom of the Father and of the Son and of the Holy Spirit". Thus we repeatedly pray in the Divine Liturgy for "unity in the faith and the communion in the Holy Spirit." Thus "communion" must not be narrowly understood as reception of a private share of the divine life through the Eucharist.

Our sharing in the life of the Trinity includes the "communion" of all other believers and we become interrelated members of the Body of Christ. This communion is equally the basis for that closer unity which must take place among the members of the community manifested in works of charity for one another. This communion among believers presupposes communion with God and, hence, incorporates it. Divine worship in the Church, then, is inherently communal, uniting a particular gathering of people with the entire Christian community throughout space and time—in fact with the entire created cosmos—through our union with Christ.

We must also be aware that celebrations of the sacraments are not completely private ceremonies. Sometimes rites such as baptisms, weddings and funerals are misconceived as pertaining only to the involved family. Each of these mysteries is, instead, the action of the whole community. They express our integration into a community of faith, the Body of Christ which is the Church.

ALL CREATION FINDS FULFILLMENT IN WORSHIP

The life in Christ involves every aspect of our being, and so divine worship *must* involve and affect all the bodily senses to focus the whole person on God. This has given rise to liturgical arts (architecture, iconography, hymnography) which, in the Eastern Churches, have been so integrated into the liturgy that they have become inseparable. And so the liturgical services of the Eastern Churches involve the whole person—spirit, soul *and* body— through gesture, music, sight and sound.

Eastern liturgical worship is designed to facilitate our presence to the reality we are celebrating, recognizing that we are creatures of both body and spirit. It is filled with meaning through words and concepts, and it affects each of our bodily senses to open us completely to God's presence. The structure of the church and the color of the icons perceived by vision reinforce our faith that we are truly present to

11

Christ and all His saints. In the Eucharist we partake of Christ's body and blood and are able to sing, "Taste and see how good the Lord is" (Ps 33/34:9). Incense reminds us through smell and sight that we are being offered to God as "a fragrant offering, a sacrifice acceptable and pleasing to God" (Phil 4:18) and that the bright cloud of the Holy Spirit is filling the temple of our worship. The sacred music of the Liturgy instills through our hearing its patterns of God's love in the depths of our being. We are creatures attuned to music which intrinsically affects us. The vestments of the ministers witness that we are all clothed in God's glory by baptism. Baptism itself physically impinges on all of our senses by the touch of hands, manifesting God's love; by the burial in water representing our death to sin; and by the manifold fragrance of chrism, giving us every needed gift of the Holy Spirit. Every liturgical celebration encompasses us totally in the saving act of God by elevating and glorifying us in both soul and body.

THE CHURCH BUILDING: ICON OF THE WORSHIPPING CHURCH

All these aspects of worship find concrete expression in the Byzantine church building. Standing before the Pantokrator, the image of the inexpressible God, we find ourselves called to bow down and acknowledge our true status before God. We are surrounded by appointments recalling both the temple of Jerusalem and its heavenly prototype (cf. Ex 25:1–27:21), but clearly focussed on the mystery of Christ at work among us. Standing shoulder to shoulder with the icons of the saints we take our place in the community of the Holy Spirit.

Some people feel that church buildings are unnecessary since God is present everywhere, even in the field under the stars. If silent prayer for communing with God were the sole purpose of the church building, this argument would have weight, as many other places would serve this purpose as well. Of course, we sometimes take refuge in our churches as places of quiet and peace for private prayer, but the true purpose of the church building becomes manifest only with the liturgy celebrated there. There are essential aspects of His presence and His relationship to us which can be perceived best in the church building as it comes alive through use. In the Church's liturgical worship God is truly acting in the midst of His people. The Lord is at work, creating us anew: salvation is a continuous happening, as the Fathers often proclaimed. Hence, in the divine services, we are present to the saving events of Christ's paschal mystery as well as to the entire Church, across time and space, which lives through His saving acts.[5] The timeless and universal effect of these events is accented when they are celebrated in a properly appointed church building representing the fullness of creation touched by the saving hand of God.

The walls of Byzantine church buildings are usually covered with icons, proclaiming a "theology in color." They follow certain traditional forms in portraying the scenes or persons depicted in order to reveal the teaching of the Church. They visually attract the beholder by expressing levels of meaning too complex for words. Icons derive from the mystery of the incarnation, in that Christ is "the icon of the invisible God" (Col. 1:15). In the incarnation God has become visible in human form, making it possible to depict Him in Christ. The style of icons reflects the transfiguration of our humanity by the divinity of Christ who is depicted as the perfect man, the model for all the other images of saints. The icons of the saints are painted according to the same principles as the icon of Christ to show deification by the Spirit into the image of God. The saints' eyes, the mirrors of the soul, are open wide to represent wisdom and spiritual insight. Their posture and clothing are harmoniously arranged to represent integrity and wholeness of being. Icons de-emphasize physical features (physiognomy) in order to lead us to a perception of spiritual reality and beauty.

The *icon screen* is the most distinctive feature of the Byzantine church structure. Its practical function is to set apart the altar area from the main body of the church (the nave). This architectural purpose of the icon screen was drawn from the style of other public structures in the Roman and Byzantine Empire. The usual division

13

between the area for the public and that for the official function was a low fence, often enhanced by columns with an architrave (a lintel running along the tops of the columns). Icons were given a more prominent place on the screen after the ninth century controversy with the iconoclasts (icon breakers) had highlighted the connection with the incarnation.

The theological function of the icon screen is to be the "gate of paradise," proclaiming that, through Christ, "the reflection of the Father's glory, the exact representation of the Father's being" (Heb 1:3), we have access to the Father and to the Kingdom of God. The icons of the Mother of God, the apostles, the gospel scenes on the screen are placed there because of their connection with the mystery of the incarnation. Likewise the Church, represented by the icons of the parish patrons, is there as the continuation of the incarnation, affording us spiritual and bodily unity with God.

The sanctuary and the nave have been given different meanings. The altar area represents the throne of God, become truly present as "our Father in heaven" who has "lowered the heavens" to dwell among us in His only Son. The nave, place of the worshipping community, signifies the pilgrim Church on its journey toward the kingdom of God. The goal of this pilgrim Church is to achieve unity with God beginning in this life and culminating in the future world. ("Thy kingdom come, Thy will be done on earth as it is in heaven.")

St. Maximos the Confessor has emphasized that both parts of the Church structure share a common purpose.[6] Maximos affirms that the structure of the church building is an icon symbolizing the unity between God and humanity, between spirit and flesh, between the future and the past, and between symbol and reality. Thus the church structure represents the purpose of the Church itself: to lead us into the presence of God, so that we can be united with Him. Through the very structure of the church building the invisible reality of the Church is presented to our bodily eyes even as we and our gifts are transformed into a heavenly reality.

14

2 — Our Sanctification in Time

The word "liturgy" refers to more than the Divine Liturgy (the Eucharist): it applies to all the services celebrated in the course of the Church's life. The term includes the *Divine Liturgy*, which is the summit of God's presence for our salvation; the *Holy Mysteries* (sacraments) which connect us with the divine life or sanctify particular moments of our lives, the *Daily Offices* which consecrate the day to the Lord, and other *occasional rites and offices* for special needs. These services transform us into sharers of the divine life and sanctify each dimension of our lives.

The existence of time reflects our limitations: it means that a human person cannot experience all of existence at once. Time marks the beginnings and ends of our earthly life. The Greeks had two words for time: *chronos* and *kairos*, which some Fathers distinguished to represent contrasting aspects of the human experience of time. These authors identified *chronos* as the measurable aspect of time, the time intervals calculated by material devices. We often yearn to escape this boundary to be united with the One who is eternal and infinite, the Lord our God. Yet God has entered time. Although immortal, He was born and died as a man. His life has now become our life; and His resurrection, our victory over death—a manifestation in time. By coming into time, God has given all time a new meaning. *Chronos*, the Fathers taught, is overcome by *kairos* (events or occasions) which means the "opportune time": for us, the "time of salvation." St. Paul proclaims the new time of Christ, "Now is the acceptable time *(kairos)*! Now is the day of salvation!" (2 Cor 6:2)

Years before the birth of Christ, the writer of *Ecclesiastes* or Qoheleth, lamented time's hold:

15

"Vanity of vanities! All things are vanity!... One generation passes and another comes, but the world forever stays.... What has been, that will be, what has been done, that will be done. Nothing is new under the sun" (Ecclesiastes 1:2,4,9).

After the Resurrection, however, we have been freed from this unremitting cycle. Time has become a vehicle for life. As St. John Chrysostom said, "There is always the same grace of the Spirit. It is always a Passover" (*Homily 5.3 on 1 Timothy*). For St. John Chrysostom every celebration of the Divine Liturgy was the saving Pasch of God, always present to us though lived out in time.

St. Maximus, too, contrasted the Old Testament vision of time with that of the New. Following the Resurrection of Christ, the times and seasons became signs of Christ's true and full presence to us at all times. As He promised, "Know that I am with you always, until the end of the world" (Mt 28:20). St. Maximus explains at length:

"[God] indicated that He Himself was to be honored symbolically through the days. For He is the sabbath, as the soul's repose after its exertions in the flesh, and as the cessation of its sufferings in the cause of righteousness. He is the Passover, as the liberator of those held in the bitter slavery of sin. He is the Pentecost, as the origin and consummation of all created beings, and as the principle through which all things by nature exist."[7]

Christ is our liberator and Savior in all things, incuding the ultimate "weapon" of time, death. "By His death," we sing , "He has trampled upon death," and has given us to share in this victory. We know we must still die biologically, but Christ has robbed death of its ultimate power. As St. Paul rejoiced, "O death, where is your victory?... But thanks be to God who has given us the victory through our Lord Jesus Christ" (1 Cor 15:55,57). For those who have been baptized into Christ, His life has become our life. We live no longer at the mercy of *chronos*, but live in the new time of Christ.

The uniqueness of this new time is that it is always fresh and opportune. Every element of Christian time is actually a celebration of the same mystery of salvation from a new perspective. The Paschal mystery of Christ's victory over death enlivens everything we do. All liturgy proclaims that Christ, by His self-emptying, has been exalted above all and raises us all with Himself. Liturgy allows us living in time *(chronos)* to see this central reality from the perspectives of all the different activities of our lives.

Three different kinds of services mark the varied ways in which we experience the ever-present mystery of Christ. Services of the first cycle mark the movement from one stage of life in Christ to another. These rites are mainly the sacramental *mysteries of the Church*. Baptism and chrismation bring us to a rebirth into the life of the Trinity. Repentance, the "second baptism," marks our passage from spiritual illness (sin) back into our baptismal life. Ordination and marriage mark new ways in which we commit ourselves to the risen Christ. Holy unction renews our life in Christ during the bodily crisis of illness. We shall explore the mysteries in more detail after the chapter on the Divine Liturgy.

The second cycle involves the rhythm of daily life. Each day is marked by various services which connect the day to aspects of the Divine Economy. Through these *daily offices* we participate moment by moment in the mystery of God's salvation and proclaim that, in the Age of Salvation, every day "... is the day the Lord has made" (Ps 117:24).

The third cycle consist of those recurring celebrations in which we remember the whole story of God's salvation through the historical events in which they happened. By these annual commemorations, we proclaim our faith that God is truly working this same salvation for us today. As previously noted, many of the Church hymns seem to celebrate a past event by beginning with the word "today," for "now is the day of salvation!" (2 Cor 6:2).

17

THE LITURGICAL DAY

The first Christian era knew two ways of calculating the hours of the day. In the Greco-Roman (civil) calendar the day was counted from midnight to midnight, irrespective of the hours of daylight or darkness. In Semitic societies each day began at sunset and continued through evening, night and into the daylight, until the next sunset. We see this in the story of creation: "God called the light 'day,' and the darkness he called 'night.' Thus evening came and morning followed — the first day" (Gn 1:5).

The Byzantine liturgical cycle incorporates both systems. On non-festive days, such as during the Great Fast and the Great and Holy Week (fasting days), the liturgical day begins in the morning and concludes with the evening services. On festivals, such as Sunday or saints' days, the daily cycle reflects the Church's Semetic roots which calculates the day from sunset to sunset. Each festival begins with vespers celebrated in the evening and ends at the Ninth Hour (3:00 P.M.) on the next day.

This shows the synthesis which occurred between the Syriac and Greek practices, as well as between the cathedral and monastic customs (see below). By the time of St. John Chrysostom, the cathedral offices of Alexandria and Cappadocia had strongly influenced the Antiochian office. Centuries later, St. John of Damascus and the monastery of St. Sabas near Jerusalem played a pivotal role in reforming the Great Typicon of the Byzantine Church.

DAILY CYCLES OF PRAYER

From the very beginning, prayer was an important part of the Christian daily life. The Acts of the Apostles tells us that the first Christians "devoted themselves to the apostles' instructions and the communal life, to the breaking of bread and the prayers" (2:42). In this they were following the example of our Lord who observed the Jewish customs of prayer in addition to His long hours of personal prayer in

18

You have made
the moon
to mark the season,
the sun
knows the time
of its setting

isolated places. The Gospels describe the vivid memories of Jesus' own prayer life which the apostles retained. The Lord also taught His disciples about the effectiveness of sincere prayers offered in faith. He even taught them a model prayer (Mt 6:9–13; Lk 11:2–4).

The first Christians were Jews who retained and transmitted their Jewish religious heritage, and so generally followed the daily Jewish cycle of prayer three times per day. They prayed in common (Mt 18:20) and in private (Mt 6:5–6). Until they were cast out of the synagogues, they probably joined the Jewish community in prayer. Subsequently, they held to this pattern of prayer (morning, afternoon and evening) and added to the traditional prayers the one taught by our Lord, the "Our Father" *(Didache* 8.3).

The basic structure of the most ancient Christian prayers themselves is based upon the Jewish way of addressing God: a remembrance of the wondrous deeds He has worked for us, a petition that He act in our behalf now, and finally a glorification of His Name. Nevertheless, Christian prayer soon began to differ from traditional Jewish prayer in a significant way. The name of Jesus came to be recognized in prayer. Jesus tells His followers, "Whatever you ask the Father, He will give you in my name. Until now you have not asked for anything in my name. Ask and you shall receive, that your joy may be full" (Jn 16:23–24 *JB*). In the epistles the pattern is to pray to the Father *through* our Lord Jesus Christ (see Rom 1:8; 7:25; Col 3:17; 1 Pt 2:5). At times prayers were even addressed *to* Jesus. In these formulas of glorification He was considered equal to the Father. These forms of prayer formed the basis for the Church's eventual definition of its belief in the equality of the Father and the Son in one Godhead. (As we pray, so we believe.)

By the second century St. Paul's injunction, "Never cease praying, render constant thanks" (1 Thess 5:17–18) would be expressed as praying to the Father through Christ. Thus Clement of Alexandria would write, "We are commanded to reverence and to honor the same One, being persuaded that He is Word, Savior, and

20

Leader, and—through Him—the Father, not on special days, as some others, but doing this continually in our whole life, and in every way."[8] This precept was fulfilled by a system of personal and communal prayer coupled with doing everything in the Lord's Name.

Byzantine monastic tradition eventually interpreted Paul's teaching to pray constantly by recommending the *Jesus Prayer*. A spiritual father explained, "The ceaseless Jesus Prayer is a continuous, uninterrupted call on [the] holy name of Jesus Christ with the lips, mind and heart; and in the awareness of His abiding presence, it is a plea for His blessing in all undertakings, in all places, at all times, even in sleep. The words of the Prayer are: 'Lord Jesus Christ, have mercy on me!'"[9] In this quotation we see the main elements of prayer: calling upon God, awareness of His presence, the opening of our selves, and the offering of our whole lives to Him. The ways to pray are numerous: publicly and privately, from the heart and from the lips, in words and in deeds, in tears and in sighs. All are necessary for prayer to be an integral part of the Christian's daily life.

THE DAILY SERVICES OF THE CHURCH

The Church's daily offices are rooted in the thrice-daily prayer services of the synagogues. Public morning and evening services are reported as being celebrated in the major Christian centers from very early times. Matins and vespers were never offices intended only for monasteries; their earliest use derives from the cathedral churches prior to the development of monastic life. They are public works, the offering of a sacrifice of praise to God in the morning and evening, an action reflected in the daily prayer of the Christian. Hence, matins and vespers came to be known as "cathedral offices," whereas the other services which fill out the daily cycle emerged later, largely in monasteries.[10]

The best witness among the Fathers to this early pattern of Christian worship was Eusebius of Caesarea:

21

"For it is surely no small sign of God's power that throughout the whole world in the churches of God at the morning rising of the sun and at the evening hours, hymns, praises and truly divine delights are offered to God. God's delights are indeed the hymns sent up everywhere on earth in his Church at the times of morning and evening. For this reason it is said somewhere, 'Let my praise be sung sweetly to him' and 'Let my prayer be like incense before You.'"[11]

Human beings naturally give thanks to God at the beginning and close of each day. *Matins* (or *orthros,* Greek for "morning"*)* is an act of the faithful to the glorification of God as the Creator of all days and times. The prayer is an outpouring of thanksgiving and praise to God who beautifies and provides for our lives. It consists of readings from the psalter, interspersed with litanies, prayers and hymns. Most characteristic of these are the canon, a poetical composition of nine odes, the psalms of praise (148-150) and the doxology.

The climax of this service, the singing of the great doxology, is introduced by the proclamation, "Glory to You [O God], who have shown us the light!" This light refers to our Lord Jesus Christ, God's only Son, who is the light of the world. For the Christian, sunrise is only a shadow, a mere symbol, of the true light of God which enlightens everyone by faith. Through its celebration of light and creation, matins (orthros) provides a natural introduction to the Divine Liturgy. It is the morning "sacrifice of praise" which is often joined to the celebration of the Divine Liturgy commemorating Him who is the Light of the world.

On Sundays and special feast days another section is added to matins between the kathisma and psalm 50. We sing psalms 134-135, called the *polyeleos* ("full of mercy"), because of the repeated refrain "for His mercy endures forever." On Sundays psalm 118 is sung with the "evloghitaria" hymns, "The choirs of angels...", recalling the visit of the ointment-bearing women to the tomb of Christ when they disco-

AN OUTLINE OF THE CHIEF FORMS OF MATINS (ORTHROS)

Sunday Matins	*Feastday Matins*	*Daily Matins*
Opening Prayers, psalms & litany	Opening Prayers, psalms & litany	Opening Prayers, psalms & litany
"Hexapsalm" (Ps 3, 37, 62, 87, 102, 142)	"Hexapsalm" (Ps 3, 37, 62, 87, 102, 142)	"Hexapsalm" (Ps 3, 37, 62, 87, 102, 142)
Great Litany	Great Litany	Great Litany
"The Lord Is God..." & troparia	"The Lord Is God..." & troparia	"The Lord Is God..." or "Alleluia" & troparia
2 Kathismata of the Psalter, hymns & litanies	3 Kathismata of the Psalter, hymns & litanies	3 Kathismata of the Psalter, hymns & litanies
Ps 117/118, Evloghitaria (resurrection hymns) and Hypakoe	Polyeleos (Ps 134-135) and Megalynarion (Slavs)	
Antiphons & Prokimenon	Antiphons & Prokimenon	
Gospel & Hymn of the Resurrection	Feastday Gospel	
Psalm 50, resurrection hymns & litany	Psalm 50 & feastday hymns & litany	Psalm 50
Canon, Canticle of Mary	Canon	Canon, Canticle of Mary
"Holy is the Lord our God" & Exapostilarion	Exapostilarion	Exapostilarion
Psalms of Praise, stichera of resurrection	Psalms of Praise, festal stichera	Psalms of Praise
Great Doxology & resurrection troparion	Great Doxology & feastday troparion	Small Doxology
Aitisis (*unless Liturgy follows*)	Aitisis (*unless Liturgy follows*)	Aitisis, Aposticha, Trisagion Prayers & troparion
Dismissal (*unless Liturgy follows*)	Dismissal (*unless Liturgy follows*)	Insistant litany & Dismissal

vered the resurrection. This is followed by an especially solemn reading of the Gospel. On Sundays this is a proclamation of Christ's resurrection; on other days it focuses on the feast being celebrated.

The celebrations of matins during the Great and Holy Week are particularly solemn. The services of Monday, Tuesday, and Wednesday—called the Bridegroom Services in some churches—include poignant calls to readiness for the coming of the Bridegroom. Friday's matins is marked by twelve readings from the passion Gospels, telling the story of the climax of Christ's saving work which led to His victory manifested in the resurrection. Saturday's matins includes the great hymns of lamentation, chanted before the tomb where the Lord's body rests while His soul finishes the work of recreation. Matins on Pascha celebrates the Lord's Resurrection with the joyful chanting of the Paschal Troparion ("Christ is risen from the dead, by death conquering death, and to those in the graves granting life."), the Paschal Canon, attributed to St. John Damascene, (based on St. Gregory the Theologian's Homily on the Resurrection), and the Paschal stichera, sung while the worshippers greet one another with the salutation, "Christ is risen! — He is truly risen!". This matins presents anew the joyful experience of the ointment-bearing women, who went to the tomb early in the morning to discover that truly Christ is risen!

The Church's evening service, *Vespers*, also celebrates a natural time of day, the setting of the sun. As darkness approaches, the Christian proclaims that Jesus is the true light of the world, the "joyful light of the holy glory of the heavenly and immortal Father." Psalm 140, coupled to the offering of incense and lighting of lamps (candles), typifies this service inasmuch as vespers is the evening sacrifice of praise. The second verse of the psalm sums up this theme: "let my prayer come like incense before you, the lifting up of my hands, like the evening sacrifice."

The first part of vespers (up to the Old Testament readings) also forms the first part of the Presanctified Liturgy, the Communion

AN OUTLINE OF THE CHIEF FORMS OF VESPERS

Great Vespers for Sunday	*Great Vespers for Feasts*	*Daily Vespers*
Opening Prayers	Opening Prayers	Opening Prayers
Psalm 103	Psalm 103	Psalm 103
Great Litany	Great Litany	Great Litany
First Kathisma of the Psalter & Small Litany	First Kathisma of the Psalter & Small Litany	Kathisma of the Psalter & Small Litany
Lamplighting Psalms & stichera	Lamplighting Psalms & stichera	Lamplighting Psalms & stichera
Entrance with "O Joyful Light", Prokimenon	Entrance with "O Joyful Light", Prokimenon	"O Joyful Light" Prokimenon
	3 Old Testament readings	
Insistant Litany	Insistant Litany	
"Deign, O Lord"	"Deign, O Lord"	"Deign, O Lord"
Aitisis & blessing	Aitisis & blessing	Aitisis & blessing
	Liti procession, stichera & litany	
Aposticha stichera	Aposticha stichera	Aposticha stichera
Song of Simeon & the Trisagion Prayers	Song of Simeon & the Trisagion Prayers	Song of Simeon & the Trisagion Prayers
Troparia	Troparia	Troparia
	Artoklasia (blessing of the bread, wheat, wine & oil)	
		Insistant Litany
Dismissal	Dismissal	Dismissal

25

rite designed to conclude fast days. When the feast of the Annunciation occurs on a fast day, the first part of vespers then forms the first part of the Divine Liturgy. This also happens on the feast of the Holy Eucharist (Holy Thursday) and on the eves of Pascha, Christmas and the Theophany. Especially solemn vesper services are held on Forgiveness Sunday, the eve of the first day of the Great Fast, when we are invited to begin the fast in the spirit of mutual love and reconciliation. Vespers on Great Friday is highlighted by the taking down of Christ's body from the cross and the procession with the holy shroud. Vespers of Pascha remembers the first announcement of the resurrection to Thomas who would not believe. The so-called "Kneeling Vespers" of Pentecost marks the return to kneeling after the paschal season.

These offices have been influenced by the monastic tradition that began in the fourth century. These monastic communities of Christians sought to follow perfectly after Christ by a life of repentance and chastity. The daily cycle of prayer in the monasteries revolved around the reading of the psalms. In their initial simplicity of life, the monks avoided singing and relied on meditatively reading a set number of psalms *(Kathismata)* in the morning and in the evening. The monasteries eventually accepted the offices of vespers and matins from the parish churches, adding sections from the psalter.

In some areas it had become customary for Christians to pray, usually privately, at other stated times during the day to fulfill better Paul's admonition to "never cease praying" (1 Thess 5:17) and the spirit of Psalm 118/119:164, "Seven times a day I praise you for your just ordinances." The monasteries devised liturgical forms to observe these *other hours of prayer.* These became the seven services during the day: Matins at sunrise, the Third Hour (at 9:00 A.M.), the Sixth Hour at Midday, the Ninth Hour (3:00 P.M.), Vespers at sunset, Compline before retiring, and the Office at Midnight, interrupting sleep. The Office of the First Hour (6:00 A.M.) sometimes followed Matins which was designed to end at sunrise. Each of these "Hours" consists of three psalms appropriate to the Hour, a prayer common to all Hours and a proper prayer for each Hour. Troparia (hymns) originally proper for each Hour are now sung only during the Great Fast.

THE DAILY CYCLE OF SERVICES

Service	Time of Day	Theme
Vespers	Sunset	Christ, the never-fading Light
Little Compline (*ordinary days*) or Great Compline (*fast days*)	Before retiring	Protection during the night
Midnight Service	During the night	The unexpected coming of the Lord
Matins (Orthros) and/or the First Hour	Sunrise	The gift of Christ, the eternal Light
Third Hour	Nine AM	Descent of the Holy Spirit
Sixth Hour	Noon	The crucifixion
Ninth Hour	Three PM	The death of Christ

Ordinarily these Hours are less solemn than the "cathedral" services of vespers and matins and are intended more for personal use. A cathedral form, including additional hymns and Scripture readings, is used on the eves of Christmas and Theophany as well as Great Friday (the Great or Royal Hours).

The First Hour celebrates the beginning of the day; whereas the other three recall the main events of our Lord's passion and glorification to remind us to take up our Cross daily and follow Christ (Mk 8:34). This self-denial and commitment to our Lord's Gospel required of every Christian, is especially the call of those striving for perfection in the monastic life. The Third Hour celebrates the Descent of the Holy Spirit at Pentecost (Acts 2:15); the Sixth Hour remembers

Jesus' crucifixion; and the Ninth Hour , His death upon the Cross (Mt 27:45). Today these hours are often combined or joined to other services in various ways. During Lent, the Third and Sixth Hours are often celebrated together as a midday service with special penitential troparia and readings from the Prophecy of Isaiah. In Holy Week, the prophecy of Ezekiel is read.

The night services are called Compline and the Midnight Office. *Compline* is said before retiring for the evening and includes prayers for a restful sleep free from sin. It concludes with mutual forgiveness among the members of the community for any wrongs, either by failures in leading the Christian life or by uncharity to one another. Some places may include a confession of faults to the superior to enable them to attain a more perfect life. Many of these traditions influenced the development of the rite of repentance for laity also.

Compline has two forms: a shorter version for ordinary days in the year and a longer one (*Great Compline*) for fast days. The character of compline is expressed in Psalm 90:5, "You shall not fear the terror of the night, nor the arrow that flies by day;" and the canticle in Isaiah 26:9–19, "My soul yearns for you, O Lord, in the night; yes, my spirit within me keeps vigil for you." Monastics also pray in the middle of the night to express the prayerful longing for God's presence expressed in this canticle. The psalmody, hymns and prayers of this Midnight Office are designed to keep the worshipper's mind on the Bridegroom and Judge who will come when He is least expected.

THE WEEKLY CYCLE OF THE CHURCH

The week of seven days goes back to very ancient times in the Middle East. Its origin may be found in nature, in the necessity for rest and the phases of the moon. In Genesis it was given a holy meaning by connecting it with the story of creation. In observing the seven day week, we imitate God who both worked and rested.

In the Jewish beginnings of the Church, the most important day of the week was the Sabbath, the seventh day. This was the holy day according to the Old Testament. It was the day on which God rested after the work of creation (Gn 2:1–3). In this passage we read, "God blessed the seventh day and made it holy, because on it he rested from all the work he had done in creation." In the Jewish faith the Sabbath was God's special day, a gift given to His people. It was a day of rest from work and for commerce with God. It was really the one day of the week in which the life of paradise was relived, the time in Eden when Adam and Eve were free from work and spoke intimately with God. Our Lord Jesus Himself died on the cross and consummated the Old Law on the sixth day, the day of the completion of creation. On the seventh day, the Sabbath, He rested after the work of recreation, even as Genesis describes the Sabbath as a day of rest after the original creation. On Holy Saturday, the hymns of the Church describe this mystery: "The King of ages, having through His passion fulfilled the plan of salvation, keeps Sabbath in the tomb, granting us a new Sabbath. ... This is the blessed Sabbath, this is the day of rest, on which the only-begotten Son of God rested from all His works" (Stichera at the Praises).

The day of Christ's resurrection was Sunday; this became a new holy day in the Church. Already in the apostolic times, Sunday, the first day of the week, became the day for the celebration of the Eucharist (Acts 20:7). Sunday was the day for the memory of the Lord and His saving work, for on this day He rose from the tomb and began a new creation. "If anyone is in Christ, he is a new creation. The old order has passed away; now all is new!" (2 Cor 5:17) Hence, Sunday came to be called the "eighth day" of the week, in that it enters a whole new time in which everything is new. "See, I make all things new!" (Rev 21:5). Sunday is the Lord's Day (Rev 1:10), the day on which God acts, the day He has made (Ps 117/118:24). It is the weekly memorial of the Resurrection, another Pascha, the first day of endless time. In some languages the name for Sunday is connected with the Resurrection (e.g. Russian *voskresenije*). At matins of each Sunday, the Church reads one of the twelve "Resurrection Gospels": readings describing the appearances of Christ to His disciples after His resurrection. The variable hymns of vespers, matins and the Divine Liturgy each Sunday are all concerned with the resurrection.

In recent years the observance of Sunday has become increasingly secularized. Attendance at church is often a matter of law or habit with no abstinence from work. The special nature of Sunday as the commemoration of our Lord's resurrection is forgotten, and the day remains only vaguely connected to religion for many Christians. Our secular life cycle often limits religious practice to Sunday morning, and the rest of the week—together with the daily and annual cycles— is unknown.

In the first centuries of the Church, the Sabbath and Sunday were observed with equal honor. The Sabbath was the holy day of rest and communion with the Lord and Sunday was the joyful celebration of the Resurrection to include the Eucharist. In the Byzantine Churches to this day, Saturday and Sunday are considered the eucharistic days without equal. Each has a separate cycle of Epistle and Gospel readings that emphasize the works of salvation of our God. As late as the fourth century, St. Gregory of Nyssa was to write, "With what eyes will you, in fact, be able to look Sunday in the face after having dishonored the Sabbath? Do you not know that these two are brothers and to do injury to one is to assail the other?"[12] When the Roman Empire officially adopted Christianity, Sunday became the official weekly civil holiday. The privilege of rest from work was transferred from Saturday to Sunday. Sunday in the Christian faith has a very beautiful and deep meaning; and its minimalistic observance in our consumer society risks loss of a great treasure of the faith.

Other days of the week acquired special commemorations. The Jewish practice observed Tuesdays and Thursdays as days of fasting. In distinction to this use, the Christians adopted Wednesday and Friday as fast days. Friday was consecrated as the day on which our Lord died on the cross. Wednesday was remembered as the day of

His betrayal by Judas. The liturgical offices of these days in current use all glorify the holy cross, and penance and fasting are observed.

THE WEEKLY CYCLE

Day of the Week	*Commemoration*
Sunday	The Resurrection of Christ
Monday	The Holy Angels
Tuesday	St John the Forerunner
Wednesday (*a fast day*)	The Precious Cross; the betrayal by Judas
Thursday	The Holy Apostles; St Nicholas
Friday (*a fast day*)	The Precious Cross
Saturday	All Saints, the rest of the departed, the original creation

Fasting in the Byzantine Church is based on the monastic model as an ideal to which the faithful aspire in proportion to their ability. It should not be an effort that would lead to pride or sloth. Rather, it should focus on our need for God's assistance in our weakness in keeping the fast or the abstinence from meat. The Great Fast (Lent) is a time for redoubled efforts at stricter observance as we come to realize more acutely our dependence on God for our spiritual growth.

Thursday was the day on which Christ revealed the Eucharist to the apostles as well as the day (Ascension Thursday) on which He sent them out to proclaim the Gospel and to baptize all nations. It has been designated as the day for the memory of the apostles. Saturday became the day for the memory of all the faithful departed being the day on which our Lord rested in the tomb. They keep the blessed Sabbath awaiting the resurrection of all. To complete the week, the remaining days were dedicated to prominent saints: Monday comme-

31

morates all the angels; Tuesday the holy prophet and forerunner of our Lord, John the Baptist; and Thursday, in addition to the apostles, also the memory of St Nicholas the Wonderworker.

3 — The Yearly Cycle

The daily cycle of prayer is closely connected with the human patterns of sleeping, rising, working and eating. The weekly cycle is similar but celebrates the ongoing events of the new creation. The Church celebrates an annual cycle of feasts as an *anamnesis* (commemoration) of the historical events which are foundational for our faith. The year represents the unit of time most adaptable for this commemoration.

The events remembered by the Church are not mere past history. These celebrations reflect our awareness of the mystery of God's love for us as manifested in the events of salvation history; but, as we celebrate them, we are actually sharing in the gift of God's love shown forth in these events. On the cross our Lord Jesus Christ, the Son of God, suffered and died in human flesh because of His love for us; but that love did not end at the moment of His death. It is as real today as it was then, allowing us to say that today Jesus is truly dying and rising for us or allowing St. John Chrysostom to say, "It is always a passover" (*Homily 5.3 on 1 Timothy*). All that God does for us He does definitively and beyond the boundaries of space and time. We are permitted a share in it through our liturgical life.

Among the annual celebrations of the Church, there are two types of commemorations. Those that occur on the same date each year are part of the *"Fixed"* or *"Immovable Cycle;* those that are celebrated on a different calendar date each year are all tied to the date of Pascha and make up the *Movable Cycle* of feasts.

PASCHA, THE FEAST OF FEASTS

The principal feast of the Christian year is the feast of Passover (in Greek, *Pascha*[13]— the English name "Easter" derives from a pagan spring festival), for the resurrection of Christ stands at the center of our faith. Though we have no direct experience of the future kingdom, our faith rests upon a real event that transformed the apostles and became the foundation of the life of the Church.

The paschal celebration is self-consciously modeled on the Jewish passover. On this day the Jews solemnly remember the event that constituted them as a nation: their liberation from the Egyptian Pharaoh and their exodus into the Promised Land under the leadership of God. Christ had given the passover a new meaning. He replaced the sacrifice of the passover lamb—commemorating the salvation of Israel from the angel of death and from slavery in Egypt—with His own self-sacrifice for the salvation of all mankind from bondage to death and sin. The parallels are astounding. In place of the lamb, Christ offered His own life upon the cross; in place of the blood of the lamb upon the lintel, the blood of Christ flowed upon the cross; instead of liberation of a chosen people from slavery to a worldly king, He accomplished the freedom from the power of slavery to sin for all humanity; and instead of the Promised Land, we were given the promise of the resurrection and life with God. The Christians began to celebrate a passover with an entirely new dimension. St. Paul can exhort his converts, "Christ our passover has been sacrificed. Let us celebrate the feast not with the old yeast, that of corruption and wickedness, but with the unleavened bread of sincerity and truth" (1 Cor 5:7–8).

The Jewish-Christians in the Middle East probably celebrated their new passover at the same time as the Jewish passover, the fourteenth day of Nisan. The Jews followed a lunar calendar causing this date to move relative to the Roman solar calendar. As the celebration of this feast developed among the Gentile Christians, it was

34

THE CYCLE OF PASCHA

Celebration	*Commemoration*	*Dates*
Pre-fast Weeks	Pharisee & Publican; Prodigal Son; Last Judgement; Expulsion from Paradise	Four Sundays before the Great Fast
The Great Fast	The 40 days of Christ's fast in the desert; the pre-baptismal catechumenate	The 40 days before the Great Week
The Great Week - Lazarus Saturday - Palm Sunday - Holy Monday, Tueday - Holy Wednesday - Holy Thursday - Holy Friday - Holy Saturday	Last week of Christ's life: - The raising of Lazarus - The entry to Jerusalem - Christ in the Temple - Anointing at Bethany - Last Supper - Crucifixion & burial - The rest of Christ in the tomb	The week before Pascha
Holy Pascha and Bright Week: "the Feast of Feasts"	- The resurrection and the appearance to the apostles	The 1st Sunday after the 1st full moon of the vernal equinox (and after the old Passover)
Paschaltide	- The presence of the risen Christ	The 40 days after Pascha
Ascension Thursday	The ascension of Christ to the Father	The fortieth day after Pascha
Pentecost	The final manifestation of the Trinity at the coming of the Holy Spirit	The fiftieth day after Pascha & the following week
Sunday of All Saints	All those glorified by the indwelling Holy Spirit	The Sunday after Pentecost

extended to three days and moved from the fixed fourteenth of Nisan to the nearest Sunday. The feast began on the Friday before, since our Lord died on the cross on Friday, rested in the tomb on Saturday (the Sabbath) and rose on Sunday. The Friday was a day of complete fast because of the suffering and death of our Lord. Sunday instead was a day of complete joy because of the Lord's resurrection. New Christians were baptized then because baptism is death to sin and rising to life in Christ Jesus.

The feast of the Pascha still retains this twofold character of a celebration of resurrection and baptism. A troparion of the Paschal Canon connects the ideas of Christ's resurrection in baptism: "Yesterday I was buried with You, O Christ [in baptism at the Vigil Liturgy on Holy Saturday]; but today I rise resurrected with You. Yesterday I crucified myself with You, O Savior. Now glorify me with You in Your Kingdom".

This feast of Pascha was subsequently expanded to a full week called the *Great and Holy Week*. The Sunday before Pascha celebrates the historical entrance of our Lord into the city of Jerusalem to enter into His passion. The previous Saturday recalles His raising of Lazarus from the dead, the event which triggered the first Palm Sunday (cf. Jn 12:9). Lazarus Saturday would become an important baptismal day in Constantinpole, to allow the neophytes to take part in the celebrations of Great Week. Holy Monday, Holy Tuesday and Holy Wednesday recall the Lord's teachings in the temple and the events that took place during the week before His arrest. Holy Thursday commemorates the giving of the Eucharist and the betrayal and arrest of our Lord. To contrast with this betrayal, it became the day for the reconciliation of those who were doing public penance.

The joyful observance of the resurrection is extended through the week after the Sunday of Pascha. Because the newly-baptized Christians wore their white baptismal robes during these seven days, it is called the *New Week* or *Bright Week*. Given St Paul's imagery of baptism as a joining of ourselves to the death and resurrection of

Christ (cf. Rom 6:3–4), it is not surprising that the annual celebration of Christ's death and resurrection became the priveleged time for celebrating mysteries of Christian initiation. Even today the Vesper-Liturgy of Holy Saturday remains the most appropriate time for baptism in the Byzantine liturgical cycle.

The celebration of the resurrection of Christ remains the most glorious experience of the Byzantine Churches. The joy of the ointment-bearing women at discovering the empty tomb of Jesus is relived in processions, music, and gestures which tell us more about the mystery of the resurrection than a thousand books or lectures.

The celebration of Pascha is the center of the movable cycle of feasts, that sequence by which we experience the meaning of Christ's gift of salvation. Periods of repentance, emptying us to feel our need for God's love, alternate with joyful celebrations of His wondrous deeds in our behalf giving us life. Immediately after Pascha, a period of fifty days—traditionally without fasting or kneeling—re-creates the time from the resurrection to the descent of the Holy Spirit (Acts 2:1–12). The fiftieth day, *Pentecost*, was already observed in the Jewish tradition as the day the Law was given on Mt. Sinai. The Christians celebrate the gift of the Holy Spirit, "for while the law was given through Moses, grace and truth came through Jesus Christ" (Jn 1:17).

The fullness of the Church with its new life in Christ comes only with the descent of the Holy Spirit who fills all things and brings this new life. This fullness of faith is expressed in the life of the Church through the various outward forms of the Tradition (the Scriptures, the liturgy, the teachings of the Fathers and Councils). None of these exhaust the expression of faith. Rather they collectively express the fullness of faith which flows from the fullness of life in the Trinity where the individual Christian must find his faith. God calls us and speaks to us in a personal way but never in way contrary to the common Tradition. Our individual faith can be understood only as a member of the Church in the context of a believing community. No one of us can possibly contain the "fullness of faith."

The Spirit mediates the presence of God in the present age, the era of the Church. He actively leads and guides the Church and individual believers. Through the Holy Spirit, Christ comes among us in the holy mysteries. Baptism and chrismation admit us into the life of the Trinity. We become God's children, are sanctified and brought to perfection.

The Church's liturgical life is a manifestation of the presence of the Spirit. In Him are we formed into the living temple of God; in Him we become a priestly people able to offer the "sacrifice of praise". The Church's liturgy is quite literally a "work for the people" and is the means by which God the Spirit works individually in our souls and collectively in the community of faith. St. Paul writes, "God is the one who firmly establishes us along with you in Christ; it is he who anointed us and has sealed us, thereby depositing the first payment, the Spirit, in our hearts" (2 Cor 1:22).

This Pascha-Pentecost period was celebrated as early as the first half of the second century.[14] It includes the feast of the *Ascension* which celebrates the return of our Lord to the right hand of the Father in glory and falls on the fortieth day after Pascha (always Thursday), according to Luke's chronology (Acts 1:3). This feast became part of the liturgical cycle after Pentecost, dating from about the fourth century.[15]

Another ancient feast of the fifty day period after Pascha is *Mid-Pentecost*, celebrated on the twenty-fifth day. It is a theological feast that celebrates the giving of life by God through the resurrection of Christ and the sending of the Holy Spirit. The readings emphasize nourishment with spiritual gifts. The Gospel for the final day of Mid-Pentecost (the following Wednesday) recounts the story of the multiplication of the loaves (Jn 6:5–14). Indeed, the whole Pentecostarion commemorates God's gift of Himself to us, filling us with life: Resurrection (Pascha); faith in Christ (Thomas Sunday); His presence in the Eucharist (Mid-Pentecost); deification (Ascension); and the gift of the Spirit (Pentecost).

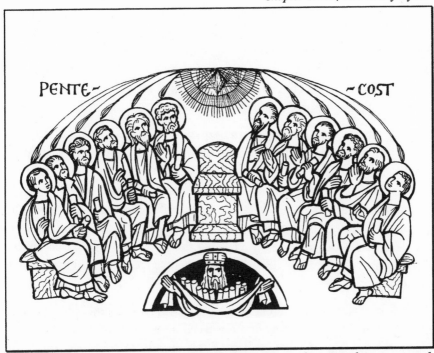

PENTE- ~COST

The icon of Pentecost clearly shows the twelve apostles are seated in a semicircle with a place reserved for Christ who may be invisibly present in the center or represented in the Theotokos, who bore Him. This icon of the descent of the Holy Spirit reveals to us the mystery of unity and diversity in the Church, born on Pentecost, much as the Trinity icon opens the mystery of unity and diversity within the Godhead.

The Apostles are gathered together in a deep inner unity in stark contrast to sin's division and confusion that reigned throughout all humanity. Pentecost is a reversal of the confusion of tongues deriving from the tower of Babel. There sin divided and scattered the people. Now, humanity is united by the power of the Holy Spirit.

Each apostle retains his uniqueness and diversity (the tongues of fire separate to alight on each unique person); yet he is bound to the others in a single new body, the Church. Once again, God reaches out to each apostle as an individual, but never in an isolated manner. Only when they gathered together in a single room, did they receive the Holy Spirit.

39

In addition to the fifty-day period of joyful celebration after Pascha, the Church has a forty-day period of penitential preparation for Pascha, called the *Great Fast (Lent)*. In the Eastern Churches Lent begins on the Monday after Cheesefare Sunday (always the seventh Sunday before Easter) and ends on the Friday before Lazarus Saturday, a period of exactly forty days.

The number forty appears frequently in the Bible as a period of preparation before the entry into a mission given by God. Moses fasts on the mountain for forty days before receiving and handing over the law to the Israelites; Elijah fasts forty days before his vision of God telling him to anoint Hazael as king of Aram, Jehu as king of Israel, and Elisha as prophet; the Israelites themselves wandered for forty years in the desert as a penance before entering the Promised Land; and Jesus fasted forty days after His baptism before beginning His public preaching.

The forty-day Great Fast of purification and preparation originated in Egypt and was first observed after the feast of Theophany (January 6). The initial purpose of this fast was the preparation of catechumens (learners) for their baptism. New Christians would be baptized at its completion.[16] This fast soon moved to its current place before Pascha and the baptism of the initiates joined to the paschal celebration.

Lent[17] was a period of instruction in the word of God, of practicing the Christian virtues of charitable works, of being integrated into the community of faith, and of fasting as a purification of body and soul for the great mystery of adoption as children of God. This special season of preparation was not restricted just to the candidates for baptism. The whole community took part, both as a sign of solidarity with those joining the Church and as a renewal of each one's personal commitment to Christ. The Great Fast, even now, is a time for us to renew our baptismal promises and our union with God. Despite (or because of) its dedication to repentance, it remains a season of great joy, a time of growing nearer to God.

40

THE IMMOVABLE CYCLE: THE FEASTS OF THE LORD

A second cycle of feasts in the Church year is called *the Immovable Cycle* because these observances are kept on the same date each year. Chief of these are the feasts of Christmas and the Theophany. *Christmas* (December 25) remembers the birth of our Lord Jesus Christ. *The Theophany* (January 6) remembers the baptism of our Lord in the River Jordan by the holy prophet John. They are closely connected because they celebrate the "appearance" of our Lord in the world. They are a development of our understanding of the identity of Jesus Christ. When He was recognized as Son of God by His resurrection (Rom 1:4), early Christians also began to appreciate this mystery of His incarnation in the Gospel events of His birth and baptism. His birth is described in the Gospels of Matthew and Luke with wise men from "the East" recognizing Him as Messiah and King and with angels proclaiming Him as such to shepherds. At His baptism John recognized Him as the great Prophet who was to come; the Father from Heaven declared Him to be His Son; and the Spirit came upon Him revealing Him to be the Messiah.

Both of these feasts have been called other "Paschas," in that the same mystery is present in both: the self-emptying of the Son of God to become a man, to live among us and to accomplish our salvation. St. Paul grasped the essence of this event and wrote, "Though he was in the form of God, he did not deem equality with God something to be grasped at. Rather, he emptied himself and took the form of a slave, being born in the likeness of men" (Phil 2:6-7).

The feast of Theophany probably dates from the third century. Before that time, only one annual feast, that of the Lord's Resurrection, was observed. This does not mean that the event of our Lord's baptism was not a part of the Gospel message of salvation, but only that the complete Christian calendar grew in history as a way of presenting the whole proclamation of the Gospel during the year of the life of the Church.

THE TWELVE GREAT FEASTS OF THE YEAR

Feast	Commemoration	Date	Duration
Nativity of the Theotokos	Mary's birth heralds the coming of Christ	Sept. 8	1 day of preparation and 5 days of the feast
Exaltation of the Precious Cross	The discovery of the cross calls everyone to worship Christ	Sept. 14	3 days of preparation and 8 days of the feast
Entrance of the Theotokos	The holiness of Mary, expressed by her entry in the temple	Nov. 21	1 day of preparation and 5 days of the feast
Nativity of Christ	The saving presence of God in the world through Christ	Dec. 25	A fast period, 2 preparatory Sundays, a five day vigil & 7 fast-free days of celebration
Holy Theophany of Christ	The manifestation of the Trinity at Christ's baptism	Jan. 6	A preparatory weekend, a 4-day vigil & 9 days of celebration
The Hypapante (Encounter)	Christ's meeting with His people when He was presented in the temple	Feb. 2	1 day of preparation & from 2 to 8 days of celebration, depending on the date of Pascha
The Annunciation	Christ is incarnate at Gabriel's word	Mar. 25	1 day of preparation & 2 days of celebration
The Entrance into Jerusalem	The coming of the Kingdom of God	Palm Sunday (*variable*)	1 day of celebration
Holy Ascension of Christ	Christ's sitting at the Father's right	Ascension Thursday	9 days of celebration
Transfiguration of Christ	Christ's glory shown before His passion	Aug. 6	1 day of preparation & 8 days of celebration
Dormition of the Theotokos	repose and glorification of the Mother of God	Aug. 15	14-day fast period, 1 day of preparation & 9 days of celebration

While many in the early Church sought to determine the date of our Lord's birth or His baptism in the Jordan, our observances of these feasts are connected more with annual calendar events than with historical dates. Their dates fall around the winter solstice, when the days begin to lengthen. All the pagan religions kept a feast around this time as a rebirth of hope in the return of the sun and warmth. Christians could not take part in the pagan festivities of false worship. Instead, they celebrated the beginning of the life of the true Son of God, the Light of Life. Thus the feast of Theophany was most likely introduced in Alexandria, Egypt to counteract a gnostic feast on the same day. Gnosticism (an early heresy) denied the humanity of Jesus and taught that the Son of God only entered Jesus at His baptism.[18] Instead, Orthodox Christians celebrated the glorification of the Lord at His baptism as a manifestation of the Trinity.

In Egypt the rising of the River Nile was of particular importance for the harvest and the life of the country. The Christians there chose the beginnings of the Gospels of Mark and John as the basis for their feast. These two Gospels begin the story of Jesus with His public life through baptism in the River Jordan. The sanctification of this river was seen as a model for the sanctification of all waters, representing life, particularly the River Nile.

While the Eastern Churches emphasized the manifestation of the Lord at the Jordan, The Western Church was to develop the feast of Christ's birth by the Virgin Mary. The Feast of Christmas originated in Rome. Since the pagan feast celebrated the lengthening of the day as a "re-birth" of the sun, the Christians chose to commemorate the beginning of Christ's life on that occasion. They celebrated the coming of the true light into the world and the birth of the Son of God. The feast existed as early as the third century.

In time most Eastern Churches would add the feast of Christmas on December 25, but retained the feast of Theophany as the celebration of the Lord's baptism in expression of the profound theology connected with it. The West was later to accept the feast of

Theophany but changed it to commemorate the "manifestation" *(epiphany)* of Jesus to the Gentile nations through the Persian wise men.

Another ancient feast combining the incarnational and redemptive themes of Christmas and Pascha dates from possibly the third century in the East. This is the feast of *the Annunciation* of our Lord (March 25). It commemorates the visit of the archangel Gabriel to Mary announcing, "The Holy Spirit will come upon you and the power of the Most High shall overshadow you... You shall conceive and bear a son and give him the name Jesus" (Lk 1:35,31). The mystery of the Lord's conception and His death bear a close connection. Both are manifestations of His love for us, His *kenosis* ("self-emptying") for our sake, by which His life and love can fill us. March 25 is important in marking the beginning of spring with new life in nature, in dating our Lord's conception in the flesh at nine months before the feast of His birth, and in being the traditional date of His crucifixion or resurrection with His "humbling Himself even to death" (Phil 2:8) for our salvation.[19]

Other feasts of the Lord were added later to the calendar. The most important of these is the feast of the *Exaltation of the Holy Cross* (September 14), clearly celebrating again the central mystery of the Christian faith. September marked the beginning of the New Year in the Byzantine Empire at about the same time as the Jewish New Year, *Rosh Hashana*. The feast commemorates the recovery by St. Helen (Constantine's mother) of the Lord's Cross when Christianity was becoming the religion of the Empire. Celebrated in Europe on May 3, the feast was kept on September 14 in Jerusalem for two reasons: first was the connection with New Year and second was the dedication of the Church of the Resurrection in Jerusalem, built by the Emperor Constantine on the sites of our Lord's crucifixion and resurrection.[20]

This feast also came to celebrate the Emperor Heraclius' seventh-century victory over the pagan Persians which liberated the

THE CALENDAR QUESTION

Since the sixteenth century the Christian world has been embroiled in the calendar question. The Julian Calendar, adopted in Rome in 45 BC was found to be inaccurate as early as the First Ecumenical Council (AD 325). Until the Muslim conquest of the Middle East in the eight century, this error was corrected on an annual basis. In 1582 Pope Gregory XIII abolished the Julian Calendar, replacing it with the Gregorian Calendar. In the Gregorian Calendar fixed dates occur 13 days before the corresponding day in the Julian Calendar. The Gregorian calendar was adopted by the Roman Catholic countries and rejected by other Western states, including Britain and its American colonies. The Eastern Churches rejected it because it caused Pascha to be celebrated with, and sometimes even before, the Jews.

Since then, the non-Catholic countries of Europe and the rest of the world have adopted the Gregorian Calendar for civil purposes. Some Eastern Churches continue to use the Julian Calendar; others employ a "Mixed Calendar", in which Pascha is computed according to the Julian and the fixed feasts are computed by the Gregorian date.

Calendar	*Paschal Cycle*	*Fixed Feasts*	*Used By*
Julian Calendar ("Old Calendar")	According to the Nicene Council	13 days after civil date (eg the Julian Dec. 25 falls on the Gregorian Jan. 7).	Many Orthodox and Greek Catholic Churches both in the U.S. and abroad.
Gregorian Calendar ("New Calendar")	According to the civil calendar	According to the civil calendar	Many Greek Catholic & some Orthodox Churches (Armenian, Finnish, Syrian, & Indian) in the U.S. and abroad.
"Mixed" Calendar	According to the Nicene Council	According to the civil calendar	Many Orthodox & some Greek Catholic Churches in the U.S. and abroad.

Holy Land. When the cross was returned to Jerusalem, it was the occasion of a great celebration. This is remembered in the ceremony of the exaltation in which the cross is elevated for veneration by the congregation.[21]

Since the cross always remembers the central act of our salvation, this feast (September 14) is traditionally solemnized in the East as a day of fasting in honor of our Lord who suffered on the cross. Special celebrations on the Saturdays and Sundays before and after the feast focus on the theme of the meaning of the Cross and emphasize its importance. They invite us to follow closely after our Lord Jesus Christ, who taught, "if a man wishes to come after me, he must deny his very self, take up his cross and follow in my steps" (Mk 8:34).

In the Byzantine Churches the date for the *Feast of the Transfiguration* is linked to the date of the Exaltation of the Cross. By tradition forty days elapsed between the Lord's transfiguration into glory on Mt. Tabor in the sight of the apostles Peter, James and John and His crucifixion. The Feast of the Transfiguration (August 6) is celebrated forty days before that of the Holy Cross instead of during the first week of the Great Fast. The Transfiguration itself has become a major event in the spiritual theology of the Byzantine Churches and deserves special attention. Human nature is revealed as glorified, deified and filled with the light of God through the dual nature of Jesus Christ who is God become fully man.

THE IMMOVABLE CYCLE: THE SAINTS

The Church also celebrates the feasts of its heroes of faith, the saints, based on this understanding of God's glorification of humanity. Through their holiness and their heroism for the sake of the faith, they reveal the ongoing action of the Spirit in the life of the people of God, deifying them and exalting them by riches of faith and love. The saints do not replace Christ as the one mediator between God and humanity (ref. 2 Tim 2:5–6). The rule of worship once again determines our faith. We ask the saints to pray and to intercede for us with God.

Their ability to help us comes only from their union with God. Just as we ask others to pray for us, we can ask those who have already achieved unity with God to pray for us. We also pray for the saints, that their share in the divine life be continually deepened. Our veneration of the saints is actually a sign of our faith in the resurrection and of the solidarity of all faithful through God. The God of Abraham, of Isaac, and of Jacob is the God of the living and not the dead (Lk 20:37–38). Our veneration of the saints is a mark of our trust in God, who always keeps His covenant with us, "so that in [Christ] we might become the very holiness of God" (2 Cor 5:21).

The first saints to be honored and venerated were those who gave up their lives physically as a witness to faith in Christ. They were called *martyrs* (from the Greek for "witness"). Chapels and altars were constructed at the site of their burial, for their death in faith and in hope of the resurrection was a special act of heroism to be honored by all Christians. This custom grew into the present practice of always celebrating the Divine Liturgy over the relics of saints. The relics are now sewn in a special cloth called the *antimension*, which is consecrated by the patriarch or bishop and given to his churches to be placed upon the altar for the celebration of the Liturgy.

Veneration of the saints is a very ancient tradition of the Church. At first, they were remembered only in the communities and places where they were buried or had given their witness to the faith. This local veneration of the martyrs' heroism spread to other local Churches. First among these saints were *the apostles*, all of whom, except for St. John, were also martyrs. The apostles had proclaimed the resurrection of the Lord and the faith they had been taught by Him which became the foundation for the faith of the whole Church. Today the greatest saint's feastday is that of the prime apostles Peter and Paul (June 29), both of whom suffered for Christ in the city of Rome. As early as the year 95, Clement of Rome was to write:

"Peter, who by reason of wicked jealousy, not only once or twice but frequently, endured suffering and thus, bearing his witness, went to the glorious place which he merited. By reason of rivalry and contention Paul showed how to win the prize for patient endurance. Seven times he was in chains; he was exiled, stoned, became a herald [of the gospel] in East and West, and won the noble renown which his faith merited. To the whole world he taught righteousness, and reaching the limits of the West he bore his witness before rulers. And so, released from this world, he was taken up into the holy place and became the greatest example of patient suffering."[22]

After the age of persecution, other classes of Christians began to be honored for their heroism on behalf of the faith. They were considered to have spiritually laid down their life for the Lord. The group included *confessors*, who suffered physically for the faith but not to the point of death; *ascetics*, men and women who renounced marriage and material pleasures for a life of penance to seek union with God; and holy *bishops*, who dedicated their lives, like Peter, to the flocks entrusted by Christ to their care. Additionally holy men and women from every walk of life were so recognized and declared saints by the Church. In the beginning each local Church did the recognizing, but later in the West a process for the discernment of holiness and the canonization of those who had become models of virtue for all Christians was developed and, in the Catholic Church, canonization of saints was restricted.

Modern Church calendars have at least one saint commemorated each day of the year. One day commemorates all saints, both canonized and unknown. This *Feast of All Saints* is observed in the Byzantine Churches on the first Sunday after Pentecost as a sign that the gift of holiness is the greatest of the charisms given to the Church through the Holy Spirit.

Besides these, each of the twelve apostles is especially commemorated: Peter and Paul (June 29), James (April 30), John (May 8 and September 26), Andrew (November 30), Philip (November

PRINCIPAL FEASTS OF THE SAINTS

Some of the saints more solemnly remembered on the calendar of the Byzantine Churches include:

Basil the Great, Archbishop of Caesarea in Cappadocia (*Jan. 1*)

Anthony the Great (*Jan. 17*)

Euthymius the Great (*Jan. 20*)

Gregory the Theologian, Patriarch of Constantinople (*Jan. 25*)

John Chrysostom, Abp. of Constantinople (*Jan. 27, Nov. 13*)

The Holy Martyrs of Sebaste (*Mar. 9*)

George the Victorious Great Martyr (*Apr. 23*)

Theodosius of the Caves (*May 3*)

Cyril and Methodius, Equals of the Apostles (*May 11*)

Constantine and Helen, Equals of the Apostles (*May 21*)

Cosmas & Damian, Unmercenary Wonderworkers (*Jul. 1*)

Athanasius of Mt. Athos (*July 5*)

Anthony of the Kiev Caves Lavra (*July 10*)

Prophet Elias the Thisbite (*July 20*)

Simeon the Stylite (*Sept. 1*)

Demetrius the Great Martyr and Exuder of Ointment (*Oct. 26*)

Barbara the Great Martyr and **John of Damascus** (*Dec. 4*)

Sabbas the Sanctified (*Dec. 5*)

Nicholas the Wonderworker, Archbishop of Myra (*Dec. 6*)

Stephen the Proto-martyr (*Dec. 27*).

14), Bartholomew (June 11), Jude (June 19), Matthew (November 16), Thomas (October 6), James the Less (October 9), Simon (May 10), and Matthias (August 9). This grouping is but a sampling of the greatest saints commemorated. It gives an idea of the great variety of lives and paths to holiness. These believers have responded to the Lord's call to be "perfect as [their] heavenly Father is perfect" (Mt 5:48). The celebration of their memory is an example for us: "Since we for our part are surrounded by this cloud of witnesses, let us lay aside every encumbrance of sin which clings to us and persevere in running the race which lies ahead; let us keep our eyes fixed on Jesus, who inspires and perfects our faith" (Heb 12:1–2).

Certain saints are celebrated for specific reasons. The *holy angels* are remembered for their role in our salvation and their constant protection and solicitude in behalf of the human race. The greatest feast of the angels is that of the Holy Archangels Michael and Gabriel and all holy angels (November 8). *St. John the Baptist*, as the Forerunner of Christ and witness of faith before Herod, is especially venerated. His unique role in regard to Christ was noted in the Gospels. Even before birth, he leapt in the womb of his mother Elizabeth when she heard the voice of Mary, the Mother of God (Lk 1:41). Our Lord witnessed of him, "I solemnly assure you, history has not known a man born of woman greater than John the Baptizer" (Mt 12:11), and he was only the forerunner of the Kingdom of God. Celebrations for John include his conception (September 23), his birth (June 24), his baptism of Jesus (January 7), his martyrdom (August 29), and the finding of his relics (February 24 and May 25).

THE IMMOVABLE CYCLE: THE THEOTOKOS

The greatest of all saints is, of course, *Mary the Theotokos*, the Mother of God. In every Divine Liturgy, the unbloody sacrifice is offered first "for our most holy, most pure, most blessed and glorious Lady, the Theotokos and ever-virgin Mary." Her position is unique in

50

salvation. As the one who by her own free will bore the Son of God in her womb, she is the first to be saved through the incarnation ("becoming flesh") of the Word of God. This is especially venerated in the feast of her falling asleep (*Dormition*) on August 15, which also celebrates her being taken into heaven (in Latin, *Assumptio*) as the first of all the human race to participate fully in the resurrection of our Lord. Other events of her life have a saving value for us as models of Christian life and because of her supreme role in the salvation worked through Jesus Christ.

These events include: her conception by St. Anne (December 9[23]), her birth (September 8), her entrance into the temple at the age of three (November 21), and finally the feast of her protection (October 1) which celebrates her role as intercessor for our behalf. She has additionally an important role in several feasts of the Lord: the Annunciation, Nativity of Jesus, Presentation in the Temple, and the encounter with the holy prophets Simeon and Anna.

Some of the data of her life are found in the Gospels and deal with her relationship to the life of Jesus. Other stories are found in apocryphal (non-canonical) Gospels, particularly the so-called *Protoevangelion of James.*[24] The Christian meaning of the feasts is based on solid tradition. Mary was indeed chosen and saved from the very beginning of her life because of her special relationship to God and in view of her call to be His mother. Her dwelling in the temple is probably completely non-historical. It does teach us the truth that the one who would give birth to Christ had become a temple of God from her infancy. God does not dwell only in a building built of stone. Mary went into the temple, though she herself was the temple of God. We, too, "are living stones, built as an edifice of spirit, into a holy priesthood, offering spiritual sacrifices acceptable to God through Jesus Christ" (1 Pt 2:5). The Church's celebration of the importance of the Theotokos stresses, not the historical events of her life, but the theological meaning of the one who bore God in her womb.

DEVOTIONAL SERVICES

Many people have been drawn through varying circumstances to a special reverence for certain aspects of our relationship with God, for the Mother of God or for certain saints. At times the presence of a saint's tomb or a historic shrine in an area has fostered these devotions. The manifestation of a wonderworking icon of the Mother of God, for example, might give rise to the desire for frequent services in her honor before that icon. In response to these sentiments, local Churches often developed liturgical services focussing on these objects of devotion. These relate to both the sacramental life and the recurring cycles of the calendar and the daily services. They are derived from or patterned on the daily worship of the Church and have become part of its liturgical tradition.

First among the Church's devotional services are those honoring Mary, the Theotokos or one who has borne God. Christians have constantly shown great love and respect to this woman who is a model of salvation and intercession. The grace of God, which "yearned to gather the children of Jerusalem as a mother bird gathers her young under her wings" (Mt 23:37), is especially manifest in her. We do not adore or worship her as God, but we do venerate her—show her reverence and honor—above all other saints. Our feelings of tenderness towards her are fitting for the Mother of our God. Through her unique role, she is a most powerful woman of prayer. Rooted in the love of Christ for His Mother, the Church unashamedly asks, "Hasten, O Mother of God, to intercede for us, O you who have always protected those who honor you!" (Kontakion to the Mother of God).

The best known devotion to the Mother of God in the Byzantine Churches is the service known as *The Paraklisis,* or "Service of Consolation". Modeled upon the office of Matins, it contains many elements of that service along with a special canon which focuses on the Mother of God as our consoler and protector. With its repeated intercessory litanies, it reflects a character of intense prayer uniting the worshippers in a concerned love for one another. The service concludes with a solemn veneration of the icon of the Theotokos, "she who shows the way" to Christ (in Greek, *Hodigitria*). In many churches this service is chanted daily during the Fast of the Theotokos (August 1–14). [25]

The celebration of this service heightens our awareness that troubles and temptations do not separate us from God's love. In Mary, a source of help and comfort, we gain a further link with the divine through her intimate connection with God as His mother. As the first saved by God, she already exemplifies that salvation means deification through the grace of our Lord Jesus Christ. Since she now rests in the deifying presence of God, we can pray to her to deliver us from all danger through her intercession. Our devotion to her is not exaggerated. It rises from the depths of our own being which carries the agony of our own inability to save ourselves. In these recesses, we receive the hope transcending our failure through what God has accomplished for her. We are able to glorify her as our protector and intercessor.

Another popular type of devotional service in the Byzantine Churches is the *Akathist Hymn*. There are a number of akathists in the Byzantine tradition, celebrating various aspects of the mystery of salvation or devotion to particular saints or icons, but the best known is the Akathist to the Mother of God. It was composed in the year 626 as a thanksgiving for the deliverance of the Byzantine capital city of Constantinople from the attacks of the (then) barbarian Slavs and Avars. "*Akathistos*" (in Greek, "not sitting") refers to the custom of the faithful to stand throughout the entire chanting of this hymn. This akathist, a series of 24 kontakia and oikoi (stanzas) in praise of the Theotokos, is prescribed to be sung during Matins on the fifth Saturday of the Great Fast. In many churches it is also sung at Compline on most Lenten Fridays, but may be sung at any time of the year as a devotion to the Mother of God. [26] The other akathist hymns follow the same basic structure.

Molebens, like the Paraklisis, are based on a shortened form of Matins. The word "moleben" itself is from the Slavonic and means a "service of prayer" directed to one theme or saint and include the following elements: Psalms 142 and 50, the singing of "The Lord is God..." with selected verses of Psalm 117/118; troparia, a Canon, New Testament readings, litanies, and a concluding prayer. Molebens may be selected from the Matins texts for any feast or saint. Common molebens are those addressed to the Lord, to His Cross, to the Theotokos or a saint, or on a theme, such as repentance. They are common services of intercession in the Slav Byzantine Churches.

One such intercessory service, popular in Slav and Greek Churches alike, is the *Lesser Blessing of Water,* which includes several series of troparia asking for the intercession of the Mother of God. It is often served in homes when special protection or deliverance is sought. Another service frequently offered in homes in some traditions is the *Service of Glorification (Slava)* honoring a family's patron saints, usually on their feastdays. It includes the blessing of bread, often stamped with the icon of the saint.

4 — The Divine Liturgy, The Fulfillment of Time

The mystery of our faith, according to St. Paul, is "Christ in us, our hope of glory" (Col 1:27), what the Greek Fathers would later call *theosis* (deification). St Paul saw this mystery as God's plan for humanity, "unknown to men in former ages but now revealed by the Spirit to the holy apostles and prophets" (Eph 3:4–5). The coming of Christ opened to us this mystery of God's plan for all humanity. In the Incarnation of His Son we see that God intended the union of all with Him through Christ. In Him we are united with God, made like Him, and restored to His friendship.

For St. Paul, this mystery fulfilled God's promise to His chosen people of salvation to the whole human race through His Messiah, the Anointed One. The people's expectation was often only political, of independence from tyrants. Christ revealed a greater mystery, freedom for all from slavery to sin and death. By the historical event of His death on the Cross, Christ reveals God's love for all humanity; and by His resurrection, He gives us the gift of freedom from sin and death. This "paschal mystery" fulfills the foreshadowing of the original passover, the exodus from Egypt.

For St. Paul only one reality existed, whether expressed in its historical events or in the commemorative symbols used to recall it. This reality was simply the person of our Lord Jesus Christ, true God and true man, dying and rising for our salvation. Every time we commemorate this mystery, the power of the Holy Spirit makes it as present to us as on its first occurrence in history. There are not two events, one real and one symbolic. Only one salvation and redemption now transcends space and time. The paschal mystery of Christ's death

55

and resurrection is especially manifest in the Divine Liturgy. Christ is here present among us as a reality, actively sacrificing Himself for us and uniting Himself to us in Holy Communion. When we join in the celebration of the Eucharist, we truly receive Christ. We are thus united to the Holy Trinity: Father, Son and Holy Spirit. We ourselves become "holy and living sacrifices, acceptable to God" (Rom 12:1). Our whole lives are transformed by the mystery of "Christ in us."

THE PASCHAL MYSTERY

Every mystery has a center, which we may call its "heart." A true mystery of faith involves our whole being: our heart and mind and soul. Mysteries seen only from the outside are mere "puzzles." Acceptance of God's invitation to enter ever more deeply into the central mystery leads to growth in understanding it, even though it can never be fully comprehended.

The heart of our Lord's life was His passion, death and resurrection. This event is the climax of the Gospels and the hour of Christ's glory (cf Jn 12:23). Each of the Gospels presents this moment as the complete revelation of God's love for us, as the fulfillment of salvation. God showed His love for us by "obediently accepting even death, death on a cross" (Phil 2:8) for our sakes, that by death He might trample upon death (cf. the Paschal Troparion).

These events in Christ's life took place during Passover, the most holy feast of the Jewish religious year. The Passover celebrated the Israelites' release from bondage in Egypt and their exodus to the promised land. The miracles God performed on their behalf to free them were remembered by means of various rituals. Most important of these was the sacrificing of the passover or paschal lamb. According to the Book of Exodus, a lamb was slaughtered by each Hebrew family and its blood smeared on the doorway. When the plague came killing the first-born son of each household, it spared those homes marked by the blood of the lamb. Death "passed over" God's chosen people.

Christ fulfilled this mystery when He Himself took the place of the paschal lamb and shed His blood on the doorpost of the Cross. He is God's first-born and only Son, whose blood saved the whole world from sin and led us all from death to life. St. Paul exclaims in joy, "Christ our Passover has been sacrificed" (1 Cor 5:7). The Gospel of St. John places our Lord's death on the Day of Preparation, when the passover lambs were being slaughtered in the Jerusalem temple, to show that Jesus fulfilled all the sacrifices of the Old Testament. This mystery expressed, "Christ entered [the sanctuary], not with the blood of goats and calves, but with his own blood and achieved eternal redemption" (Heb 9:12). Here was fulfilled St. John the Baptist's prophetic identification of Jesus at the beginning of His ministry, "Here is the lamb of God" (Jn 1:36).

All four gospels as well as St. Paul tell us how, just before His death, Christ celebrated a "last supper" with His apostles: a meal the evangelists are careful to present in the context of the Jewish Passover. Jesus took bread and wine and identified them as His body and blood. He gave us a new ritual to celebrate: one that is not merely symbolic but real, freeing us from the death of sin whenever we participate in it with faith. Henceforth whenever we would receive Communion, we would be truly united with Christ both in our body and our spirit. We therefore call the bread of the Divine Liturgy the "Lamb." The Eucharist is truly our Lord, the Lamb of God, the One who suffered, died and is risen, the perfect fulfillment of all sacrifices.

The Eucharist *is* the Body and Blood of Christ, the gift from the heart of His passion and resurrection. Both as elements and as action the Eucharist is Christ; who died and rose for our salvation. The Eucharist is a truly "Divine" Liturgy, because it is a mighty work of God undertaken for our sanctification. When we partake of it, we are made one in Christ and united with God: Father, Son, and Spirit. It is called a mystery since the way in which it happens is beyond our comprehension. Nevertheless, by participating in it with faith we can grow continually in our understanding of God's great love for us.

"But when Christ came as the high priest of the good things to come, then through the greater and more perfect tent (not made with hands, that is, not of this creation), he entered once for all into the Holy Place, not with the blood of goats and calves, but with his own blood, thus obtaining eternal redemption" (Heb 9:11–12).

THE NEW COVENANT

The Gospels make it clear that the Lord Jesus Himself made an explicit connection between the breaking of the bread and the sharing of the cup at the Last Supper, and the sacrificial offering of His life that would take place the next day through the breaking of His body and the shedding of His blood. Christ gave the mystery of the Eucharist as the basis for a new covenant between God and His People: "This cup is the new covenant in my blood, which will be shed for you" (Lk 22:20; 1 Cor 11:25). This "covenant" refers to the solemn agreement on Mt. Sinai between God and His people: God agreed to be the God of Israel, and the people agreed to keep His commandments. A new covenant had been foretold in a prophecy which the Byzantine Churches prescribe to be read on Holy Saturday, "This is the covenant which I will make with the house of Israel after those days. ... I will place my law within them, and write it upon their hearts" (Jer 31:33). This new covenant is the perfect gift of God's love for us expressed in the coming of the Messiah, Jesus, the Word of God incarnate, who joined the fullness of the divinity with the perfection of humanity.

By partaking of the Eucharistic mystery, we enter into this new covenant with God: not an external agreement between two parties, but a union which makes us truly a new people sanctified by His Word. In it we are truly united with God and able to join in the one sacrifice which is able to transform us and make us holy.

"DO THIS IN MEMORY OF ME"

The mystery of the cross and the resurrection is one with the mystery of the Eucharist: the ratification of the new covenant between God and humanity. Whenever we celebrate the Divine Liturgy God's work in Christ becomes our own. At the Last Supper, our Lord commanded us to repeat what He had done, "Do this as a remembrance of me" (Mt 28:19). At the Liturgy, we fulfill this command when the priest—raising the chalice and diskos in the form

59

of a cross—prays in the name of the people, "Remembering, therefore, this salutary command[27] and all that was done in our behalf ... we offer to You Yours of Your own." Our oblation and the Lord's sacrifice are the same, differing only in the way in which it is offered. On the cross Jesus offered His life in a bloody sacrifice, and in the Liturgy we enter into His offering through our sacrifice of praise. The terms used in the Divine Liturgy itself for our participation in Christ's sacrifice are "spiritual worship," "unbloody, rational sacrifice," "a sacrifice of praise." This kind of worship was revealed by the Lord in His comments to the Samaritan woman, "An hour is coming, and is already here, when authentic worshipers will worship the Father in·Spirit and truth. ... God is Spirit, and those who worship him must worship in Spirit and truth" (Jn 4:23–24).

The Liturgy is an *anamnesis* (commemoration) of the death and resurrection of the Lord. While this commemorative ritual calls to mind the reality of Christ's love for us on the Cross and in His third-day resurrection, it actually makes this love present here and now. St. John Chrysostom explains, "Christ is our High Priest, who offered the sacrifice that cleanses us. Now we also offer that which was once offered, and which cannot be exhausted. This is done in remembrance of what was then done, for He said, 'do this in remembrance of me' (Lk 22:19). We do not offer another sacrifice ... but we offer always the same, or rather we perform a remembrance of a sacrifice."[28]

The Divine Liturgy has a double nature like the dual nature of Christ, who is both God and man. The Divine Liturgy is a commemoration of an event which took place in a particular space and time, the death and resurrection of our Lord. This connection with a unique event of human history gave the Liturgy certain symbolic interpretations. Thus the Great Entrance has been likened to the burial procession of Jesus or His Palm Sunday entrance into Jerusalem. The preparatory rite at the table of prothesis has been likened to the birth and hidden childhood of Jesus; and the Little Entrance with the Gospel Book, to the preaching of our Lord. These symbols have helped the piety of the faithful in attending the Liturgy, but they do not convey the full richness of meaning. The Liturgy is more than simply a commemoration. As the deeds of our Lord are remembered, they are also truly present in a mystical way. The Fathers could thus call the Liturgy a "logical," or "rational," or "unbloody" sacrifice in that the event recalled is truly present, though unperceived by our senses in its true reality. The love of God for us on the Cross, in the tomb and through the resurrection is really present to us today. It is a true sacrifice whose mystery has been revealed and is expressible without being fully understood.

The Divine Liturgy is one action which is, at the same time, both symbol and reality. Its symbolic nature does not make it any less real. When we present these rites and words, when the bread and wine are placed on the holy table and consecrated, we experience this amplified reality as "Christ is among us." We are forged together as Church in a sanctifying action which frees us from sin and fills us with the Spirit in the fullness of the future kingdom experienced in the present. When we eat and drink the Body and Blood of Christ, we unite with God in the Holy Trinity through the Word who became flesh for our sake. St John Chrysostom declared this mystery, "For it was not enough for [Christ] to be made man, and to be struck and slaughtered, but He also commingles Himself with us, and not by faith only but in very deed, He makes us His body ... and we are made one body and one flesh with Christ."[29]

How the commemoration of a sacrifice once offered can be the sacrifice itself is possible only through the power of the Holy Spirit. St. John of Damascus says of the Eucharist, "Just as God made all that He made by the operation of the Holy Spirit, so also now the operation of the Spirit performs those things that are above nature and which it is not possible to comprehend except by faith alone."[30] By the Spirit Mary conceived Jesus; now by the Spirit our Lord is present in the holy mystery of the Eucharist and accomplishes what His death and resurrection means for humanity. If the Divine Liturgy were merely

THE DIVINE LITURGIES OF ST BASIL & ST JOHN CHRYSOSTOM

First Section: Preparation of the Clergy	*Second Section: Preparation of the Gifts*	*Third Section: Enarxis (Assembly Rite)*	*Fourth Section:Service of the Word*
Prayers before the Doors	Cutting of Lamb	Great Incensation	Little Entrance, Troparia
Washing of Hands	Preparation of the Chalice	"Blessed is the kingdom..."	Trisagion
Vesting	Arranging of the Particles	Great Litany and Prayer	Prokimenon, Epistle
	Veiling & Censing	Antiphons	Alleluia & Gospel
	Prayer of Offering	Little Litanies and Prayers	Homily
		Hymn, "Only Begotten Son"	Litanies

Fifth Section: Service of the Eucharist

Pre-Anaphora	*Anaphora*	*Pre-Communion*	*Communion*
Great Entrance	Thanksgiving	Litany & Prayer	Communion of clergy & people
Litany & Prayer of Offering	Anamnesis	Lord's Prayer & Prayer of Inclination	Hymns, Litany & Prayer of Thanksgiving
Peace	Epiklesis	Fraction & Mingling of Lamb	Prayer at Ambo
Creed	Commemorations	"I believe, Lord, and profess..."	Blessing & Dismissal

our calling to mind of past events, these events would indeed remain simply images and symbols. By the working of the Holy Spirit, our offering of praise becomes the one sacrifice pleasing to God. St. John Chrysostom observes, "We indeed offer, but by making a remembrance of [Christ's] death, and this remembrance is one and not many. ... Christ is one everywhere, being complete here and complete there also, one Body" (op.cit.).

THE ANAPHORA

The central part of the Eucharist, the *Anaphora* ("Prayer of Offering"), begins with the blessing of the priest, "The grace of our Lord Jesus Christ, and the love of God the Father, and the communion in the Holy Spirit, be with all of you" (cf. 2 Cor 13:13). It ends with the doxology (glorification) by the priest, "And grant that we, with one voice and one heart, may glorify and praise Your most honored and sublime Name—Father, Son and Holy Spirit—now and ever, and forever." To this the congregation responds, "Amen!" ("So be it!").

The anaphora is based on the Jewish prayers of blessing *(barakoth)*, a typical example of which is "Blessed are You, O Lord, King of the universe, who bring forth bread from the earth."[31] At the Last Supper, Jesus said such a prayer of blessing over the bread and wine of the meal. Jewish blessings begin with a solemn address of God which mention His relevant attributes. A narration would follow of all the appropriate good works God has done for us. As God is blessed for His past deeds, He similarly acts for us now through the mystery of His unchanging love for us. The prayer closes with a supplication that God accomplish here and now this same blessing for us.

The Byzantine anaphora of St John Chrysostom begins with a solemn address to God the Father, who is "ineffable, inconceivable, invisible, incomprehensible, ever existing, yet ever the same." These same attributes are applied to the whole Trinity: Father, Son and Holy Spirit. The prayer then enumerates all that God has done for us, proclaiming our faith in a loving God who saves us. He not only made us

63

but continually provides for us: "You brought us forth from nonexistence into being, and raised us up again when we had fallen, and left nothing undone, until You brought us to heaven and bestowed upon us Your future kingdom" (Anaphora of St. John Chrysostom). The Liturgy is not only a commemoration of past events; it is also a celebration of the future destiny of the human race.

The highpoint of God's saving work for us is the sending of His Son. This is the central theme of the Anaphora of St. John Chrysostom, which in turn quotes the Gospel's own expression of ultimate love, "God so loved the world that he gave his only Son, that whoever believes in him may not die but may have eternal life" (Jn 3:16). The priest's recital of Christ's earthly life and work ends with the account of the Last Supper in which our Lord told His disciples to eat and drink, for, "This is my body ... This is my blood."

In the *anamnesis* which follows we solemnly proclaim that we remember all that Christ has done for us, in order to fulfill His "salutary command" ("Do this in rememberance of me"). For God, all of time is an eternal present. As limited creatures, we are constrained to experience time as a succession of events. Whenever God acts, all of salvation is accomplished. With the psalmist we are always able to sing, "This is the day the Lord has made, let us be glad and rejoice in it" (Ps 117/118:24). When Moses led the Israelites through the sea, he prefigured our freedom from sin's slavery by the baptism of Christ "in water and in spirit" (Jn 3:5). When the Lord fed the Hebrew people in the desert with manna, He prefigured the living bread we would receive in Holy Communion (Jn 6:32–33). When the Lord fed the multitude with the multiplication of loaves and the wedding guests with wine from water, he prefigured His gift at Holy Communion. He also demonstrated His lordship over the elements of creation that daily feed us. The Divine Liturgy makes all the past of our salvation present today, and it also makes the future present. Today the final justification of all mankind is already present and we are able to "remember" the "second and glorious coming again." Every celebration of the Liturgy is an expression of our faith that God is already accomplishing His promises!

The *anamnesis* is joined with a gesture of offering. The deacon lifts the Holy Gifts as the priest says, "We offer to You Yours of Your own...." Here an identification is made: we offer the created gifts of bread and wine given to us by God the Creator. As we remember Christ's saving command, the priest implores the Father to send the Holy Spirit to transform the Holy Gifts (*epiklesis*). The elements become the true Body and Blood of His only Son, who indeed belongs to Him. The anaphora concludes with prayers for the living and the dead and for the needs of all.

The goal and completion of the Divine Liturgy is Communion: unity between God and humanity and unity among the believers. We pray in the anaphora to join those partaking of the consecrated gifts to have "communion in the Holy Spirit." The Liturgy unites God and human beings cooperatively (in Greek, *synergy*). The divine part is the work of salvation accomplished in Christ's death and resurrection. The work of the Holy Spirit mysteriously makes our ritual action the manifestation of God's love for us. The anaphora addresses the Father, "[who] so loved Your world that You gave Your only-begotten Son, that everyone who believes in Him should not perish, but should have life everlasting" (citing Jn 3:16). Our part is the offering of the gifts: bread and wine from our hands, a sacrifice of praise from our lips, the remembrance of Christ with our minds, and our expression of love for God and one another from our hearts. We lift up our hearts; we remember; we offer. Yet God is the One who loves and "remembers," making the past events real today. He both "offers and is offered" (Prayer of the Cherubikon). He sent His Son; He created the gifts of bread and wine; and He makes them His Son as the "real, heavenly bread" (Jn 6:32).

THE EPICLESIS

The anaphora continues with the *epiclesis* or invocation of the Holy Spirit. Priests are ordained in order that they might pray to the Father in the name of the whole community for the Spirit to act among the people. God, who accomplishes all His work of salvation through the Spirit, completes the Liturgy through this same Spirit. As St. John Chrysostom explained, "[The priest] who is present does nothing, nor is the right accomplishment of the offered gifts due to human nature, but the grace of the Spirit being present, and coming down on all makes complete that mystical sacrifice."[32]

The priest calls upon God to:

"...send down Your Holy Spirit upon us and upon these gifts lying before us. Make this bread the precious body of Your Christ and that which is in this chalice the precious blood of Your Christ, changing them by Your Holy Spirit, that to those who partake of them, they may be for the purification of the soul, for the remission of sins, for the communion in Your Holy Spirit, for the fullness of the heavenly kingdom, for confidence in You, not for judgment or condemnation" (Anaphora of St. John Chrysostom).

The goal of the Eucharist, as expressed in the epiclesis, is the sanctification of the people taking part in the Divine Liturgy. The Liturgy is a gift for our sanctification, our being raised up from sin and being made like God (deification). The first step in the process of sanctification is the forgiveness of sins. Sin is the consequence of misusing free will. It robs us of freedom. The human race has had an inclination from the beginning to sin, to lose the gift of freedom. Hence, the world is under the power of sin. The destruction of sins and the reestablishment of freedom can be achieved only by a life patterned on the obedience of Jesus to His Father. The power and strength to be purified of sin is a gift of the Holy Spirit to His Church (Jn 20:22–23) and is made manifest especially in the Divine Liturgy. The first petition of the epiclesis is for the *"purification of the soul, and the remission of sins."*[33]

The Divine Liturgy is celebrated, in the words of the epiclesis, *"for the fullness of the heavenly kingdom."* This may be understood in two ways. The first is the reestablishment of God's kingdom in this world, by the death and resurrection of Jesus the Lord as promised, "Among those standing here there are some who will not taste death until they see the reign of God established in power" (Mk 9:1). The mystery of the Liturgy is the ritual celebration of an already present reality, "Christ in us, our hope of glory" (Col 1:27). When we sing the Cherubikon, for example, we "mystically represent" the Cherubim, who sing to God's glory in the heavenly court; but since Christ is truly present in the celebration of the Liturgy, the church becomes in reality the "heavenly Jerusalem," establishing God's power in the world.

In the second sense, however, the kingdom has yet to be fulfilled. When Christ tasted the cup of His passion to destroy the power of sin, He told the disciples, "from now on I will not drink of the fruit of the vine until the coming of the reign of God" (Lk 22:18). The meaning of the death and resurrection of Christ for our history is yet to be revealed even though the event itself is the fullness of God's salvation and the fount from which God transforms the world. The future will be revealed as we live according to the way of Christ.

The choice of Sunday as the Lord's Day is itself a sign of this twofold dimension of the Kingdom. Sunday is both the day of the resurrection of our Lord (commemoration) and the day on which Christ has been expected to come again. Sunday is the day of New Creation: the resurrection makes all humanity new and God's will for all creation will one day be fulfilled.

The Eucharist brings the gift of *"communion in the Holy Spirit."* This phrase is used repeatedly in the Liturgy to signify both union with God in the Trinity and union with one another in fellowship (in Greek, *koinonia* means both communion and fellowship). Reception of Christ in the Eucharist is meant to deepen the unity we have with other believers in the Church as fellow children of the Father, the temple of the Holy Spirit, and the Body of Christ (cf. 1 Cor 3:16; 12:27).

"Unite all of us who share the one Bread and the one Cup with one another in the communion of the Holy Spirit" (Anaphora of St. Basil the Great). Truly living out this communion would transform the world and attain humanity's destiny. Human differences make living in fellowship difficult; but the pattern of Christ's sacrificial life and the power of the Holy Spirit show us the way and enable us to do it. This is the greatest blessing of the Liturgy: it is the chosen means by which God makes us worthy as "a chosen race, a royal priesthood, a holy nation, a people he claims for his own to proclaim [His] glorious works" (1 Pt 2:9), in a unity of faith and love.

LITURGIES OF THE BYZANTINE TRADITION

The mystery of the death and resurrection of our Lord is celebrated by Christians according to Jesus' command, "Do this in memory of me" (Lk 22:19). All Christians who celebrate the Eucharist do so according to a basic format given by the Lord. The Liturgy is rooted in the tradition of the Jews from whom the Messiah came. However Christ's command, "Make disciples of all nations" (Mt 28:19), would lead to adaptation to great cultural diversity while preserving the basic truth of the gospel, including the Eucharist. Despite changes in different places and ages of Christian history, the Liturgy is still recognizable as the Christian outgrowth of a Jewish synagogue service with scripture reading and the prayer of *barakah* (blessing).

The most ancient elements of the Liturgy are the prayers addressed to God, such as the *Eucharistic Prayers* or anaphoras, which include elements of blessing, praise, glorification and thanksgiving. The Eucharistic Prayers of all historic Christian Churches follow the basic lines of these Jewish prayers of blessing or consecration, often with a lyric thesaurus such as this: "It is proper and just to sing hymns to You, to bless You, to praise You, to thank You, to worship You..." (Anaphora of St. John Chrysostom).

Throughout the course of the centuries, each particular Church has developed its own form of the Liturgy, while continuing to express the same universal theme. They all witness to one another and to the faith of the people of God as expressed in their worship. The Assyrian, Coptic and Syrian Churches have a number of Eucharistic Prayers in their traditions, while the European traditions (Byzantine and Roman) have been more conservative. Thus, from the sixteenth century until the Second Vatican Council the Roman Church had only one Eucharistic Prayer, the "Roman Canon." Then three more were added which follow ancient and traditional forms. The Roman fourth Eucharistic Prayer, for example, is generally based on the Coptic Anaphora of St. Basil.

In general the Byzantine Churches use two anaphoras. The first and more frequently employed one is that of St. John Chrysostom.[34] This anaphora is a more developed form of the Syrian Anaphora of the Twelve Apostles. It did not originate in the Byzantine capital of Constantinople and was likely introduced there by the Syrian, St John Chrysostom, when he became its archbishop. It is not, as was often thought, a shortening of the Anaphora of St. Basil. Rather the Anaphora of St. Basil comes from the Cappadocian tradition of Asia Minor. This anaphora is much longer than that of St. John Chrysostom and contains a wealth of Scriptural passages beautifully woven together to describe the whole work of salvation. It is not a penitential anaphora and originally was used for all Sundays and great feasts. Today, it is limited to the five Sundays of Lent, Holy Thursday, the vigils of the feasts of Pascha (Easter), Christmas and Theophany and the Feast of St. Basil (January 1). Most of the Eastern Churches have some form of the Liturgy of St. Basil, which has had great authority among them. St. Basil himself, or at least his immediate disciples, were responsible for the Cappadocian form which was accepted in the Church of Constantinople.

The Liturgy of St. James is also used by some Byzantine Churches. The Liturgies of St. John Chrysostom and St. Basil share the same Constantinopolitan format with variant prayers. The Liturgy of St. James, in contrast, has an entirely different structure which derives from the Church of Antioch. The Anaphora of St. James was the traditional Eucharistic Prayer of the Church of Jerusalem.[35] Though it certainly does not date back to St. James himself, it is very ancient and highly respected by the churches of the East. The Liturgy of St. James, retained for certain occasions by the Melkite Church, reflects the traditional ties of the Church of Antioch with Jerusalem. This Liturgy has also been used at various times in the Greek Church and it has also been translated into Church Slavonic.

THE PRESANCTIFIED LITURGY

The Liturgy of the Presanctified Gifts is one of the most characteristic services of the Lenten season. It consists of vespers to which a Communion Service has been added. It does not have an oblation or an anaphora and so is not a complete celebration of the eucharistic Liturgy. An anaphora commemorates our Lord's resurrection. In the Gospel story of Christ's appearance at Emmaus, we see that the disciples "recognized" the Lord when "he took bread, pronounced the blessing, then broke the bread and began to distribute it to them" (Lk 24:30). This four-fold action is certainly the celebration of the Eucharist, and in the Gospel story we see that the Christian faithful always discover the risen Lord in the celebration of the Divine Liturgy.

The whole season of the Great Fast (Lent) has a different symbolism. Here instead of celebrating the Resurrection, our prayers, fasting, almsgiving and acts of penance symbolize the forty year journey of the people of Israel through the Sinai desert to the Promised Land. The "Promised Land" of the Christian is the Resurrection of our Lord giving the fullness of life to all who believe in Him. The Byzantine Churches came to consider it inappropriate to pray the anaphora on the weekdays of Lent and formulated another service, "revealed by the God of unspeakable and invisible mysteries" (Prayer Before the Our Father). It consists of an entrance with the Holy Gifts that have been consecrated the previous Sunday, and their distribution in Holy Communion.[36]

By celebrating this Liturgy of the Presanctified Gifts, we proclaim our faith in Jesus as "the real heavenly bread... [which] comes down from heaven and gives life to the world" (Jn 6:32–33). Lent represents the passage from Egypt to Israel, the promised land. On this journey God's people were fed miraculously by the manna from heaven. During our Lenten journey, we are fed with the heavenly manna that gives life. As the Lord explained, "Your ancestors ate manna in the desert, but they died. This is the bread that comes down from heaven for a man to eat and never die" (Jn 6:49–50).

Today the Liturgy of the Presanctified Gifts is prescribed for Wednesdays and Fridays of Lent, though originally it was celebrated every day of the Great Fast, including Good Friday.[37]

5 — The Holy Mysteries: Sanctification of Life

The concept of mystery, at its source expressing the whole plan of the Creator for His universe, has become applied by the theology of the Church to certain embodiments in rite and word. Baptism, the Eucharist and the other sacraments are known as *the holy mysteries* of the Church. They do not replace the broader relationship between God and humanity. While remaining signs, they become the reality of that relationship in a way that transcends our senses. No purely intellectual search for God exists for He has already found us and unites Himself to us in ways beyond human understanding. The unbeliever may see only ritual gestures; the faithful gaze into the underlying reality. St. John Chrysostom explains this in relation to baptism:

> It is called *a mystery* when we do not consider what we see, but see one set of things and consider another. ... Here the judgment of the believer is one thing, while that of the unbeliever is another. For myself, I hear that Christ has been crucified, and at once I marvel at His love for humanity.... The unbeliever, hearing of a bath, thinks it only water; I, on the other hand, consider not only what is seen, but the purification of the soul by the Holy Spirit.[38]

This central mystery of new life in Christ is variously manifest in different moments of our lives. All of the Church's mysteries are ways in which God acts in our lives through symbolic gestures and words. Through them the grace of the Holy Spirit is conferred, according to the faith of the Church. In another sense all the sacraments are united as a single "seven-fold" mystery of Christ's presence. The Church as the Body of Christ forms the center of this one mystery. Here God and man are truly united.

The most fundamental of all sacraments is thus the Church itself. The Second Vatican Council said this quite clearly, "The Church, in Christ, is in the nature of sacrament — a sign and instrument...of communion with God and of unity among all men."[39] All the sacraments are initiated by the Church and within the Church. A necessary requirement for each is the faith of the Church and the intention to celebrate this mystery according to the mind of the Church. Each of the holy mysteries is necessarily an action of the Church. The Church is the extension throughout history and the whole world of the mystery of God becoming man for our salvation. When the Church acts, Christ is acting through the Holy Spirit; and when we are joined in the Church, we are united with God and deified.

In addition every mystery has an "ecclesial dimension" relating it in some way to the Church. Baptism and chrismation admit us into the Church and invest us as members of the royal priesthood. The mystery of repentance (confession) allows the penitent to be forgiven and reconciled to the Church in order to receive Communion with it.[40] The mysteries of priesthood and crowning (marriage) designate Christians to minister to the community of believers, either the Church or the domestic church, the home. Even holy unction presumes the involvement of the worshiping community whence all healing flows from the presence of Christ, the Physician of both body and soul.[41] In testimony of this each mystery is fulfilled by or oriented to the great manifestation of Christ and His Church which is the Divine Liturgy. As St. Simeon of Thessalonica was to write, "Holy Communion is the perfection of every sacrament and the seal of every mystery."[42]

THE MYSTERIES OF INITIATION

The mystery which gives us an entrance into the life of the Holy Trinity and participation in the presence of God in His Church is baptism. After baptism we are no longer natural children, but children of God by grace. We become brothers and sisters of Christ as adopted children of the Father, filled with the strength and love of the Holy

Spirit. We are part of the Body of Christ, His Church; and we receive all the rights and responsibilities of membership in it.

Baptism is a gift for both the individual Christian and the whole Church. The person is rescued from the pattern of Adam's disobedience and renewed by Christ's consistent obedience to His Father. God desires more than just the salvation of individuals. He wants the salvation and re-creation of His whole world. Every baptism expresses each one's willingness to do the right as an individual; but it also proclaims the establishment of the kingdom of God in the whole world. Christ gave the Apostles their mission, "Go, therefore, and make disciples of all the nations. Baptize them in the name of the Father, and of the Son and of the Holy Spirit. Teach them to carry out everything that I have commanded you. And know that I am with you always, until the end of the world" (Mt 28:19–20). Baptism is a sign of the presence of God's reign as well as His future glory. We commit ourselves (with our own voices or through our godparents) to this truth by reciting the Creed as our profession of faith and by baptism in the name of the Trinity.

All sacramental mysteries consist of verbal and nonverbal imagery, of gestures and of prayer. In baptism the whole person—body, soul and spirit—is sanctified using physical matter which has been set aside as holy. And so, after the profession of faith, the water used in baptism is consecrated by a solemn prayer. Water cleanses, refreshes, and is essential for life. As such it is a symbol of rebirth, of life. Water also carries an element of death, of destruction. Water, which parted for the Chosen People fleeing Egypt, drowned their masters. And so it also represents death: the burial and resurrection of Jesus. In the Paschal Canon we sing, "Yesterday I was buried with You, O Christ [referring to the baptisms on Holy Saturday], but today I rise, resurrected with You." .

The water and the person to be baptized are then prepared by an anointing with olive oil. This oil used for the pre-baptismal anointing recalls the twig of the olive tree given to Noah "as a sign of reconciliation and deliverance from the flood." The dove with an olive branch was a sign to Noah in the ark of his reconciliation, the covenant of peace, between God and humanity. The baptismal "oil of gladness" is a sign for us that our reconciliation in Christ is imminent. This oil is also considered "an armor of righteousness"[43], recalling the struggle of repentance that comes with accepting the new life in Christ.

In the Byzantine Churches baptism itself is conferred with the words, "The servant of God (*name*) is baptized in the Name of the Father, and of the Son and of the Holy Spirit. Amen." The form of baptism (in Greek, *baptizo* or "to submerge") is patterned on that of our Lord by the prophet John, thereafter called "the Baptist." Christ descended into the water as a sign of repentance, though He had no need of repentance, and was revealed to be the Son of God by the voice of the Father and the manifestation of the Holy Spirit in the form of a dove *(theophany)* . Our Lord gave a new significance to John's baptism, "I baptize you in water for the sake of reform, but the one who will follow me... will baptize you in the Holy Spirit and fire" (Mt 3:11). Christian baptism not only cleanses us of our sins, but also gives life in the Spirit as a new creation.

Baptism is a celebration of the Paschal mystery. Our descent into water symbolizes our going into the tomb with Christ. Our ascent from the font represents the resurrection of our Lord. The two-fold nature of baptism as a cleansing from sin and a new life in the Trinity is expressed in various ways. The baptismal epistle states, "Through baptism into His death we were buried with Him, so that, just as Christ was raised from the dead by the glory of the Father, we too might live a new life... in the same way, you must consider yourselves dead to sin but alive for God in Christ Jesus" (Rom 6:4,11). Before baptism, therefore, the Christian must solemnly renounce evil in the form of Satan and commit totally to Christ.

After baptism, a white robe—the garment of righteousness (cf. Is 61:10)—is put on to contrast with the nakedness before baptism. The baptismal garment, the "robe of light", indicates that we have been

SAINT CYRIL of JERUSALEM

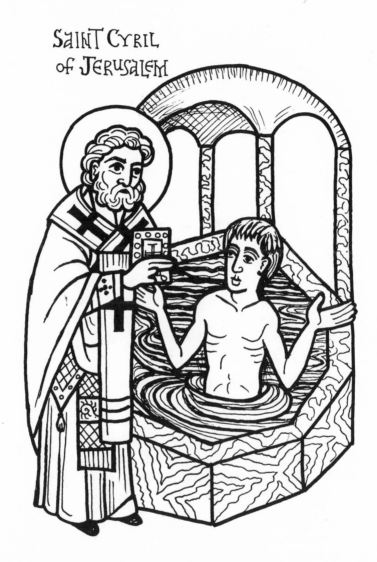

During Bright Week Saint Cyril of Jerusalem explained the meaning of the mysteries of initiation to those who has received them on Holy Saturday. His five "Mystagogical Catecheses," which describe a rite almost identical with that of today, are among the most precious testimonies of the early Church.

clothed in Christ (Gal 3:27), replacing the shame of Adam and Eve at their nakedness apart from God (Gen 3:27). Their attempts to cover themselves with leaves reflected their choice which made them dependent on the material side of creation with its slavery to passions and to death. The baptismal garments, already alluded to in Revelation 3:18 and 7:13,14, represent the return to Paradise and reveal man's true nature restored in God's image and likeness.

When we are baptized into Christ, we put on Christ. We are literally immersed in Christ, who also leads us to the Father and gives us the gift of the Holy Spirit. Only in Christ can we come to know the Father, for no one has ever seen the Father except the Son (Jn 1:18), and only He can lead us to the Father since only He truly knows the way (Jn 14:5). Only in Christ do we become children of the Father, adopted sons and daughters, heirs of the kingdom.

The rite of initiation is actually a twofold mystery: baptism "in water and the Holy Spirit" (Jn 3:5). We die to sin in Christ that we might rise to life in Him, but we are also "sealed by the Holy Spirit." Through Christ we also receive the Holy Spirit, who seals our baptismal initiation. Just as the feast of Pentecost completes the Paschal feast, and as the descent of the Holy Spirit completes the commissioning of the disciples, so our chrismation, our reception of the gift of the Holy Spirit, completes our baptism.

At His baptism in the Jordan River, Christ was revealed as the Messiah (in Greek, *Christos* or "Anointed One") by the descent of the Holy Spirit in the form of a dove. At our baptism, we are anointed with holy chrism, olive oil impregnated with many fragrances to symbolize the manifold gifts of the Spirit, and called by St Cyril of Jerusalem the "antitype of the Holy Spirit."[44] This chrism is solemnly consecrated by the primate or the local bishop following the anaphora in the Liturgy of Holy Thursday. Initially the bishop, as head of the local Church, celebrated the initiation of every adult. This relationship with the bishop is preserved by reserving the consecration of chrism to the head of the Church.

THE CHURCH'S SACRAMENTAL LIFE

Rite	*Prinicpal Elements*	*Significance*
Baptism and Chrismation	Exorcisms, renunciation	Deliverance
	Profession of Faith	Commitment to Christ
	Anointing with oil	Joy and strength
	Baptism in water	Union with Christ
	New clothing	Heavenly apparel
	Anointing with Chrism	Seal of the Holy Spirit
	Elements of the Liturgy (Readings, Eucharist)	Heavenly nourishment for the journey of life
Eucharist	*(see chapter 3)*	*(see chapter 3)*
Repentance	Public Service (hymns, prayers, readings)	Communal nature of our life in Christ
	Private Confession before icon of Christ	Opening of the heart to Him
	Imposition of hands & priestly stole with prayer	Church as the "hands of Christ"
Holy Unction	Office of hymns, prayers & readings	"The prayer of faith will save the sick"
	Anointing with blessed oil	The medicine of faith
	Imposition of open gospel book	Church as the "hands of Christ"
Crowning	Exchange of rings	Lasting commitment
	Exchange of Crowns	Call to stewardship
	Procession	Call to priesthood
	Common Cup	Sharing of all things
Priesthood	Imposition of hands	Passing on of ministry
	Vesting	Signs of office

The priest anoints the person's forehead, eyes, nostrils, mouth, ears, chest (heart), hands and feet with the words, "The seal of the gift of the Holy Spirit!" This indicates that we are indeed "Christians," "anointed ones" together with our Lord. This sealing expresses the mystery of our election and salvation by God, for "in him you too were chosen; when you heard the glad tidings of salvation, the word of truth and believed in it, you were sealed with the Holy Spirit who had been promised" (Eph 1:13). This new relationship with God and with the Church carries the responsibility of faithfulness to the truth: "As his anointing teaches you about all things and is true — free from any lie — remain in him as that anointing taught you" (1 Jn 2:27).

The model for the rite of baptism and chrismation is found in the Gospel accounts of our Lord's baptism. We imitate Jesus by our baptism in water and our anointing with holy chrism. Just as the Holy Spirit revealed Jesus to be the "Christ" after His baptism, we are revealed to be "Christians" by our chrismation following our baptism. Only by this gift can we truly respond in faith and call God our Father. Only the presence of the Holy Spirit within us can lead us to discern God's presence and to respond to that presence. Chrismation fills us with the power of the Spirit to do what is right and to repel evil.

Our baptism into the life of the Trinity is completed only when we join in the Eucharistic communion with the rest of the Body of Christ. Baptism gives us entrance into the life of Christ; Holy Communion makes that membership full and perfect: "if you do not eat the flesh of the Son of Man and drink his blood, you have no life in you" (Jn 6:53). Each reception of Communion is a renewal of our baptism, showing our faith and hope in Christ by re-committing ourselves to the true and holy. We are then able to sing, "Keep us in sanctification that we may sing Your glory, meditating on Your righteousness all the day."[45]

REPENTANCE: "THE SECOND BAPTISM"

Baptism signifies our complete break with "the old man." The candidate must renounce all evil and make a commitment to Christ. The early Church was quite emphatic about being faithful to this commitment. In some places, for example, there was no return after apostasy from the way of Christ: "If we sin willfully after receiving the truth, there remains for us no further sacrifice for sin" (Heb 10:26). Yet Our Lord had taught us the mystery of forgiveness as àn ongoing process. The disciples were taught to forgive each other repeatedly: "seventy times seven times" (Mt 18:22). The early Church saw a distinction between the "daily sins" of even the most committed believer and a more dramatic or decisive renunciation of Christ and His way. It included prayers for forgiveness of the "daily sins" in most of its services, but restricted reconciliation from serious sins in a solemn way.

The Church forbade the repetition of baptism but allowed the forgiveness of subsequent sins by a separate rite, the mystery of Repentance. The absolute renunciation of sin made in baptism could not be compromised, yet God's mercy could welcome back those who stumble and fall on the road of life if they were truly repentant. In the first centuries of the Church, this mystery was performed publicly. It consisted generally of a public admission of sin, exclusion from the worshipping community during the performance of an adequate penance, and eventual absolution through the imposition of the bishop's hands. The Fathers often termed this mystery of repentance the "second baptism." Origen explained the difference between the forgiveness of sins in baptism, which was gratuitous and complete, whereas the forgiveness of penance required much tears and labor.

After official persecution of Christians ceased during the age of Constantine (fourth century), Christianity became socially popular and eventually the official religion of the empire. These changes diluted the sense of commitment of the ordinary member, but gave rise to a new elite, those in the monastic life. Monastics practiced regular, even daily, confession—not only of public scandals—but of all sins, transgressions, and spiritual weaknesses. As this practice spread throughout the Christian world, the Irish Church—which had experienced a tremendous flowering of monasticism—seems to have been the first to permit private confession to a single representative of the Church. The priest, as an official of the Church, began to hear confessions privately and was required never to reveal to anyone what he heard, directly or indirectly, even under the threat of death. Today the rite of this sacrament may consist of a preparatory public service, private confession of sins, a spiritual exhortation, a penance given by the priest, and the prayer of forgiveness (absolution) by means of the imposition of hands.

The faithful began early in the Church to use penance in two ways as the practice of private confession spread. The first was still the reconciliation with God and His Church for grave sins committed after baptism. At baptism God completely forgives our sins, which we renounce, giving us access to Communion with Him and making us members of His Body, the Church. This union is broken when we turn away from Him and commit a serious sin. Before we can return to Communion, we must seek reconciliation with the Church by the confession of the offense through a true *metanoia* (change of mind). This mystery restored the penitent to the life in Christ as a full member of His body and is completed only with the reception of Holy Communion, the fount of all forgiveness.

A second use for this mystery was as a means for eradicating, not only immediate sin, but the tendencies toward sin impeding spiritual progress. The confessor came to stand in the role of one's "spiritual father" or "healer." The state of the penitent's soul had to be revealed to the priest to show not only the serious sins but also the faults and the sins of weakness. The priest could then give spiritual direction and guidance in leading a fuller Christian life.

This practice indicates that the believer, though completely freed from sin through baptism, requires a continuing nurture of grace to allow growth toward maturity in Christ. It initiates us into a life-long reality of living in God as His adopted children. We live out our baptismal commitment daily whenever we turn from what is wrong and do what is right. Maturation in learning to choose the good is an apt description of the Christian way. Gregory of Nyssa writes, "Human perfection consists precisely in this: constant growth in the good."[46] Having chosen the right road of life does not eliminate stumblings and errors. Participating in the mystery of repentance enables us to continually adjust our sights to the right path as we as we walk toward enlightenment and fullness of life.

Both of these options are still available for use, but they are used less frequently than in the past. The reasons may be a lessened sense of sin, a greater ethos of individualism, or bad experiences with the sacrament from either shame or an insensitive confessor. Nevertheless, the constant mission of the Church is to preach and to encourage repentance and forgiveness. Indeed, "the Church has never failed to call people from sin to conversion and by the celebration of penance to show the victory of Christ over sin."[47]

MYSTERIES OF CONSECRATED SERVICE

Marriage was a gift of God to humanity from the very beginning. By creating men and women, God made for each a companion, a helpmate to share the joys and burdens of life. Through marriage, a man and woman are able to go beyond themselves. They become one new person and share with God in the process of creation by bringing new human beings into life and raising them in God's image. In the Church, marriage is even more: it is transformed into a kind of priesthood of service and an icon of the saving love of God by being consecrated by Christ and drawn into His paschal mystery.

The reason Christian marriage is considered a mystery of faith may be found in the epistle of St. Paul as is read at the marriage ceremony, "[Marriage] is a great mystery; I mean that it refers to Christ and the Church" (Eph 5:32). The committed love of a man and woman is the most intense human love there is. It is a singular image of the relationship between God and the human race. In the Old Testament, God revealed Himself to His people Israel as their bridegroom, "I will espouse you to me forever; I will espouse you in right and in justice, in love and in mercy" (Hos 2:21). In the Gospels, John the Baptist testified that Jesus was the Messiah, the bridegroom of the Church. John proclaims, "I am not the Messiah, I am sent before him. It is the groom who has the bride. The groom's best man waits there listening for him and is overjoyed to hear his voice. That is my joy and it is complete" (Jn 3:28–29). The mystical marriage of Christ and His Church is best represented by the Cross, where for the love of His people, the Son of God gave up His life. In the mystery of marriage, two people likewise give up their own lives in a complete commitment to one another, to become one new person. Each marriage, therefore, is a personal manifestation of the mystery of God's love for all.

Because Christ is God made man, marriage is no longer the same reality. It has now acquired a divine dimension since in it the spouses become like God. In marriage separate but equal persons become one, according to a particular order, yet without their individuality being obliterated. In this a Christian couple is an icon of the Trinity, where Father, Son and Holy Spirit are one in essence yet distinct in person.

In the Eastern Churches, the central ritual gesture of this mystery—from which it takes its name—is most appropriately *the Crowning*, for in this way the man and woman are revealed as being lifted up to a special share in God's life. They fulfill the promise of the psalmist, "You have made [them] little less than the angels and crowned [them] with glory and honor. You have given [them] rule over the works of your hands' (after Ps 8:6–7). This passage indicates that the married couple share again in the role of Adam and Eve as stewards of the creation prior to their fall into sin.

The Christian couple is called to fulfill the priestly nature of human race. As every person fulfills his nature in worship, the Christian couple fulfills its nature by caring for their segment of the world and offering it to God. This is represented in the rite of crowning when the couple are led around the sacramental table in procession. As they walk, the same hymns are chanted as are heard in the rite of priestly ordination.

The mystery of crowning, as is true of baptism, is not simply a ceremony but a new relationship, one which touches all aspects of each person to open them to the possibility of true intimacy. It is this intimacy, more than romance and sex, which is at the heart of a profound human need. This mystery implies that the recipients must come to share their lives in a way that can build a community of true love, open to the possibility of growth into family through participation in the creative process.

Marriage is a life-long commitment of a man and a woman to each other. The Church does not accept divorce because our Lord taught, "let no man separate what God has joined" (Mt 19:6; Mk 10:9). The Church does set aside marriages if an unbelieving spouse refuses to live with a believer for the sake of faith (cf 1 Cor 7:15). The Church may also declare null a marriage that was defective from the beginning. This can happen when by reason of lack of ability or for other serious grounds, one or both partners are unable to make the commitment required by the marital relationship.

The various orders of the clergy participate in the mystery of Christ and His Church, which is God's gift of His very self to His people, in a unique way. While all Christians are called to build up the Body of Christ, the clergy have that service as their very reason for being. At the same time, while the entire community celebrates the Eucharist, the clergy are its ministers in a unique way. While the center of this mystery is service at the Holy Table (for the Eucharist is the center of God's presence in His Church), those ordained serve the Church in all aspects of its life. Persons chosen for these offices must

84

be outstanding servants of the people and must be called to this service and be confirmed by the grace of the Holy Spirit.

It is proper that those who are thus called to serve the Liturgy and the Church should be consecrated by a special mystery. In this sacrament a person is accepted into an order of service to the Church by the laying-on of the bishop's hands. This imposition of hands identifies this person as especially chosen for this service. At the same time it imparts to him the grace of the Holy Spirit for the fulfillment of his ministry.

The mystery of *Priesthood* is always celebrated within the Divine Liturgy because the center of the ministerial character is service at the Eucharist. Three orders of service to the altar are constituted in this mystery: bishop, priest and deacon. The ritual gesture for the conferring of each order is the same laying on of the bishop's hand. As overseer of all service in the Church, only the bishop may ordain. The candidate is led in procession to the bishop, who exchanges the kiss of peace with him. The candidate then kisses the Holy Table at which he shall serve. As he kneels at the corner of the altar, the bishop imposes his hand upon the candidate's head and proclaims his ministry by the words, "Divine grace, which heals all and supplies what is lacking, promotes (*name*) to the (episcopate *or* presbyterate *or* diaconate)." Two prayers are then said with the bishop's hand still imposed asking for the gift and working of the Holy Spirit. The rite is completed by the vesting of the newly-ordained in the garments of his office and the proclamation, "*Axios*" ("He is worthy").

The fullness of orders is possessed by the bishop. He is the "High Priest," the father and shepherd of the community. As head of the Church, he presides at all liturgies, either personally or by assigning a priest as his representative. The bishop (in Greek, *episkopos* means "overseer") has the pastoral care of the whole Church and must supervise its daily life to lead it to the fullness of God's reign. In his ministry he is the successor of the apostles in the sense of having the highest authority in the Church. He presides over the local church entrusted to his care and may join with the other bishops in council (synod) to exercise responsibility over the wider Church as well. Because of the great responsibility of the bishop's office, his Church prays for him by name at practically every divine service. Today he is usually selected from among the priests for this office.

The priest is the servant of the Church who serves on the parish level. Because of this, he has the closest daily contact with the people. The original meaning of the word "priest," was "presbyter" or "elder." The priest was a wise man of the community, chosen to give counsel to the bishop and to represent the people. When the Churches grew too large for the bishop to be everywhere and to administer every parish directly, he appointed his closest advisors, the priests, as his deputies. By the bishop's authority and the imposition of hands, the priest presides at all divine services (except ordinations), administers, teaches and counsels the faithful given to his care.

The priest is particularly a man of prayer. His office in worship is to lead the whole community in prayer, to which it joins its "Amen." This office of prayer also manifests itself in preaching, explaining the word of God which has been proclaimed. The priesthood is a total commitment to Christ's Body, the Church. It thereby shares in the Paschal mystery of Christ's dying and rising. The priest dies through his giving of his life to the people and rises to the glory of life in intimate fellowship with God.

The third major order is that of deacon, which means "servant" in Greek. The office of deacon is linked to St. Stephen and the others who were chosen to serve the material needs of the Greek-speaking community in Jerusalem, thus freeing the apostles to proclaim the word of God (Acts 6:1–6). Stephen is recorded as a great preacher, "filled with grace and power, who worked great wonders and signs among the people" (Acts 8:8). He became the first martyr for the faith, the first to follow in Christ's footsteps by witness to the death.

The particular mark of deacons is to imitate Christ as servants of the Church: "The Son of Man has not come to be served but to serve — to give his life in ransom for the many' (Mk 10:45). The first deacons worked closely with the bishop in the administration of the diocese. During worship they stood at his right and maintained the proper order of the service: proposing the petitions for prayer (litanies), guiding the celebrants and giving instructions to the people. They also administered the charitable works of the Church. These included taking care of the poor and the sick and providing for the burial of the dead. They assisted the bishops and the priests in counselling the people. They were usually the first to hear cases and guided them to the right solution. The early Church considered the diaconate as the order most closely patterned after Christ's earthly life of service. In Rome, the deacons were so important that the archdeacon of the city was usually elected Pope. For many centuries in some Churches women were ordained as deaconesses and performed similar tasks for women of the community.

In the later centuries, the order of the diaconate began to decline, though it has always remained stronger in the Eastern Churches than in the West. The Second Vatican Council recommended the restoration of this order in the Catholic Church.[48] The restoration of this office since then has proceeded in both the Eastern and Western Catholic Churches. Its revitalization has begun to increase the number of ways believers in these communities can be of service to God's people.

A MYSTERY OF HEALING

Baptism, the mystery of our new life in Christ, proclaims His victory over sin and death. The sin of Adam had brought suffering and death into our world, but the death of Christ on the Cross was seen as a victory over death. Death was the end result of man's dependence on the material side of his existence, of seeking short term expediencies instead of trusting God. By Christ's obedience to the Father, the

Source of life, He reversed the Fall and opened for us a way to share in His victory.

Because of Christ's victory, biological death no longer has spiritual power over us. Yet we continue to fall victim to the physical power of sickness and death, even as we remain subject to the decaying influences of time and space on our material bodies. Sometimes illness is the direct or indirect result of our own sinful behavior. As such, it should impel us to repentance. At other times our physical afflictions are the result of the actions of others and reflect mankind's freely chosen vulnerability to the devil's deceits.

Whatever the cause, physical illness is usually accompanied by a weakening of the spirit. Sufferings—especially afflictions for which we are not directly responsible—tend to destroy the victim in spirit as well as in body. Growing through suffering is barely possible for the strong; most experience spiritual as well as physical loss when afflicted with serious illnesses. The resulting need for forgiveness and healing through the mystery of Christ's death and resurrection is the reason the office of *Holy Unction* or *Anointing* of the sick is one of the seven sacramental mysteries of the Church.

The Epistle of St. James instructs Christians, "Is there anyone sick among you? He should ask for the presbyters of the church. They in turn are to pray over him, anointing him with oil in the Name of the Lord. This prayer uttered in faith will save the one who is ill, and the Lord will restore him to health. If he has committed any sins, they will be forgiven" (Js 5:14–15). This anointing is a reaffirmation of our baptismal victory in a time of spiritual and bodily crisis. Our faith in this anointing is that it will forgive sins and cure the illness of soul to permit a healing of the body to proceed. Thus spiritual healing does not reject whatever material aid that medicine can provide in dealing with suffering in all its dimensions. Rather it is directed to reviving our confidence in Christ's victory over sin and death in the midst of our suffering so that we may find new opportunities for growth and restoration of wholeness within.

Holy Unction is the most intense prayer of the Church for those who are ill. It emphasizes not impending death, but hope in God in times of affliction, as Psalm 142:11 proclaims, "For the sake of your name, O Lord, You will keep me alive; in your saving bounty, you will deliver my soul from oppression." In its full form, this service is modeled on the morning office of the Church with the singing of a Canon for the one who is ill. Olive oil is then blessed with an invocation of the Holy Spirit. Readings from Scripture proclaim the good news of Christ's victory over sin and death. The sick are repeatedly anointed on the forehead, eyes, ears, nostrils, lips, chest, hands and feet with a solemn prayer addressed to the Father. These anointings should be administered by more than one priest, but often this is not possible. Indeed, at one time it was so prescribed because St. James referred to "presbyters" in the plural. The rite concludes with the laying of the holy gospel book on the sick person's head as a sign of the forgiveness of sins.

Like the other mysteries, holy unction is a solemn and public prayer of the Church. Although administered by the priest, all the faithful should be present and join in this prayer. Usually after anointing, Holy Communion is given as the completion and perfection of every mystery, permitting forgiveness and healing to flow from our union with the Trinity through the Body of Christ.

The nature of holy unction has been misunderstood in Church history. It has at times been considered as the "last rites" and in the West was even given the name "Extreme Unction." The faithful did not request it except when convinced that the hour of their death was imminent. Even today many are reluctant to ask for this mystery, regarding it as spiritual strength for the final journey. The Second Vatican Council moderated this view somewhat, "'Extreme Unction,' which may also and more fittingly be called 'Anointing of the Sick,' is not a sacrament for those only who are at the point of death. Hence, as soon as anyone of the faithful begins to be in danger of death from sickness or old age, the fitting time for them to receive this sacrament has already arrived."[49]

In the Eastern Churches the goal of this mystery is rather to reaffirm our faith and bring us forgiveness and healing. This is why holy unction is not given primarily to those in danger of death, but to any who are sick. In some Churches it is offered to all during Great Week for the healing of our spiritual ills in preparation for Pascha. The "Last Rites" of the Church actually consist in the giving of Holy Communion as one's provision (Latin, *viaticum*) for the road to eternal life, along with prayers at the departure of the soul from the body.

OTHER MOMENTS OF SANCTIFICATION

The seven mysteries of the Church described above have a special place in the life of a Christian. The Eucharist signifies the continual presence of our life-giving God and Lord, and the other rites mark entry, growth, renewal and service in our life of faith. These seven mysteries have certain elements in common: they were given us by God through the Body of Christ; they celebrate some aspect of His dying and rising for us; and they all manifest His presence among us in His Body. The seven mysteries represent a symbolic perfection, the union of God (the Holy Trinity) with the four elements. Though we no longer especially value numeric symbolism and no longer recognize only four fundamental elements of matter, the sacraments do represent for us the complexity of ways in which we are united to God in our journey through life. The number of mysteries does not correspond to the number of different rites. Two mysteries, baptism and chrismation, are meant to be celebrated together. There are three distinct rites of ordination: to the episcopate, the priesthood and the diaconate.

The Roman Catholic Church holds as faith that there are seven sacraments (Council of Trent). The Orthodox Churches, though never defining it, have accepted this tradition by recognizing the same mysteries as sacramental. Most Protestant communities accept only two, as having been directly instituted by our Lord (Baptism and the

Eucharist). The seven mysteries or the seven-fold mystery rests clearly on the presence of Christ in His Church. Other actions of faith also manifest some aspects of God's work in His Paschal mystery.

The Church at various times in its history has recognized other offices as having a special importance in the life of a Christian. Though they may not be recognized as one of the seven, nevertheless they are "sacramental" moments. Foremost among these are funerals and the making of a monk or nun. *Funeral and memorial services* mark our passage from this life. They are characterized by hymns which acknowledge death as the last vestige of the "old man" in us and prayers for forgiveness, which are the last expressions of repentance celebrated by the Church for the departed.

Some Eastern Churches preserve the ancient tradition of anointing the dead at the end of the service, recalling the solemn anointing with olive oil prior to baptism as a sign that the person who has died in Christ is united with Him in His death and in the hope of resurrection. "Then [at baptism] the sacred anointing summoned the initiate to a holy warfare; now the pouring of the oil signifies that in this combat he has fought to victory."[50] While some of the Fathers had considered the funeral service a sacrament, their opinion is not universal, perhaps because the faithful person for whom we pray has passed beyond the signs of this world.[51]

Becoming a monk or nun was also considered by some Fathers as a special consecration and a second baptism. St. Simeon of Thessalonica (fifteenth century) accepted the system of seven sacraments, yet still included the rite of *the consecration to monastic life* under the mystery of repentance. The faithful Christian man or woman chooses to seek perfection by the giving of self entirely to Christ in fulfillment of His command, "If anyone wishes to come after me, he must deny his very self, take up his cross and follow in my steps" (Mk 8:34). The monastic life, through its poverty, chastity and obedience, is a particular and marvelous sign to the world of the power of Christ's death and resurrection. It is a life of sacrifice, yet fulfilling

91

the promise of Christ: "Your souls will find rest, for my yoke is easy and my burden light" (Mt 11:29–30).

The Church has also considered as sacramental moments *consecrations and blessing* of things connected with our sanctification. These visible manifestations of God's redemption of the whole world are signs to us of the power of His death and resurrection. Tradition has not regarded them as sacraments because they are not in themselves a rite or entrance into the Paschal mystery. They are connected with it as instruments given by God who wishes the salvation of all. Most important among these is the *consecration of a Church.* By faith we know that God is "present everywhere and fills all things;"[52] yet we know that we are not ordinarily sensitive to this presence. We need reminders of the heavenly dimension which surrounds and upholds us. The church building becomes for us a sacred space, a visible icon of the kingdom of God. Our worship becomes a sacred time wherein we come collectively into God's presence to be united with Him and each other for our sanctification. The church structure, therefore, is given a special blessing or consecration by the bishop. It is almost a kind of baptism to mark this place as a special one where the Lord acts, a portal into the Kingdom of God. The Church also celebrates rites of blessing over all the items used in liturgical worship—icons, vestments, sacred vessels, altar cloths, reliquaries, palms, candles—each of which shares in the function of the church building. The consecration of some of these materials— the altar, the holy chrism, and the water sanctified on Theophany— were considered by some Fathers as particularly important sacramental moments.

Special blessings of food are conducted in conjunction with the festal observances of the Church. On the Great Feasts five loaves of bread, recalling Christ's multiplication of the loaves, are blessed and shared during the vigil, along with wheat, wine and oil are blessed (the *artoklasia* or "breaking of the bread"). On Pascha those foods not eaten during the Great Fast (meat, eggs, cheese) are blessed and eaten.

"O Lord Jesus Christ our God, who blessed the five loaves in the wilderness, and thus sutained five thousand men, bless these loaves with this wheat, wine and oil, and multiply them in this holy place and for Your whole world..."

(Artoklasia)

Other blessed foods are specifically connected with festal observances: the paschal bread called the Artos (Gk: bread), recalling the mystery of Christ's sacrifice, grapes—to be "transfigured" into wine and the blood of Christ—on the feast of the Transfiguration of Christ, and, in some traditions, wine and specially inscribed breads on the feasts of the saints.

Numerous elements of daily life are traditionally blessed, bringing them into our life in the Kingdom of God. There are special prayers or services connected with the home (on laying the foundation, on moving into the home); with vehicles, or with businesses: traditionally agriculture (lands and implements, barns, herds, or on planting and harvesting), beekeeping (bees, hives), or fishing (nets, boats, stocking ponds). There is no aspect of proper human activity which cannot be sanctified by prayer and the committed stewardship of faithful Christians.

6 — Living Liturgically

The Christian must be a person of piety: one of the most esteemed virtues of the early Christian world. St. John Chrysostom calls piety, "a pure faith and a moral life" *(Homily* 12.2 *on 1 Timothy)*. Clement of Alexandria accounts piety as the highest of all virtues, "it is clear to everyone that piety, which teaches to worship and honor, is the highest and oldest cause" *(Stromata* 2.18). Many of the hymns of the Church honoring the saints praise their piety. However, piety in this perspective means true faith and righteous conduct. The pious Christian is a person who worships "in spirit and in truth" (Jn 4:23) and who acts justly toward each person.

True piety is not a weak virtue whose practitioners wear sad expressions and downcast eyes. Real piety cannot be counterfeited, falsified or feigned: it must be genuine and honest. Since one of its qualities is true faith, it must be in line with the proven tradition of the Church. It includes righteousness in conduct, meaning always seeking justice and charity for all. Piety not founded on true faith and justice cannot be called piety at all.

Unfortunately, piety sometimes appears overly sentimental under the pressure of the individualism of the age in which more weight is given to personal feeling than to sound belief. Religion under those conditions comes to be thought of as something completely subjective in which dogma is secondary. Emotion doubtlessly plays a significant role in our religious life, but it must be guided by reason. A movement within seventeenth century German Lutheranism was called Pietism. It represented a sincere attempt to correct problems of faith, but emphasized devotion over right dogma. Its effects have been felt in Protestantism to the present day with indirect effects in other churches in the United States.

95

Authentic Christian life integrates correct teaching, proper liturgical expression, profound emotion and mutual love. Faith in God cannot be merely detached intellectual assent, but is meant to be an affair of the heart. Our approach to liturgical worship, then, should be one of piety: a heartfelt giving of ourselves to God through the experience of the divine services.

LITURGICAL EXPRESSION

A basic dimension of liturgical piety involves an ability to express, through communal words and gestures, our relationship to God, which is both deeply personal yet rooted in the Tradition. To be fully human requires communication. We realize that something would be very wrong with a person who never spoke to another either by words or signs. As rational beings we use words to convey meaning, ideas, feelings and emotions, our desires and loves, and our perception of the beauty we see in the world around us. Often we find that our own words are not sufficient to express those aspects of our deepest selves which we seek to share with one another. This is when humans invariably turn to ritual.

Ritual is natural to human communication as we attempt to express the ultimate mystery of our existence. Through ritual we communicate to one another our deepest beliefs and goals. All human beings must ritualize in some way. Even when a person has lost all faith, he or she will still attempt in some way to communicate meaning to life through various kinds of words or gestures. For believers, this meaning is expressed in our liturgical rites, which reflect our acceptance of life as a gift from God who gives it meaning in the depths of our hearts.

The basis of our liturgical worship, then, is the expression of our relationship with God through ritual. It makes an offering of our words of praise, communicating in its ritual gestures and words our self-offering to God in Christ. The raising of our hands, our prostrations to the ground, our constant repetitions of "Lord, have mercy" or "Christ is risen" express on a more basic, almost instinctive level what learned texts proclaim through developed thought. Liturgical piety assumes that the worshipper is comfortable with this kind of expression.

Another side of liturgical worship is its repetitive character. While there is some variation in the services according to the seasons or feasts, liturgical prayer is largely the same each day. Liturgical piety, then, rests on a conviction that it is by constant repetition of prayer, rather than by variety of prayers, that the heart is drawn to God. Just as we grow in faithfulness by keeping the same commandments over and over, we grow in the spirit of the liturgy by the repetition of its prayers and egstures.

Liturgical piety also presumes that we perceive God the Word communicating with us and drawing us to the truth through the words and gestures we use in our liturgical prayer. The Church's liturgical tradition is a vehicle through which the Holy Spirit works to perfect our offering of praise. As the composition and collection of the Scriptures was accomplished through the power of the Holy Spirit, likewise the Church's liturgical life is inspired by the presence of God. Through it we not only communicate but are united with God. The events of His salvation take place within us. Believers imbued with liturgical piety become "disciples" in worship, seeking to learn from the divine services the mystery of God's dealings with us.

God's communication of Himself in the liturgy is something unique, but it is not magic. We can begin to understand how God is acting in our lives through its prayers and rites even without fully comprehending what He is doing for us. Liturgical ritual can be analyzed and explained from various scientific or sociological viewpoints, but cannot be fully assimilated except through faith. For this reason, one of the conditions for the fruitful reception of any of the sacramental mysteries has always been the presence of faith. St. Gregory of Nyssa wrote that if we are not really changed by baptism (i.e. if our faith is not real), "[then] the water is but water, for the gift of the Holy Spirit in no way appears in him who is thus baptismally born."[53]

We live in a pragmatic world that promises quick rewards, entertainment or stimulation. As a result, many people today have a difficulty with a liturgical worship which does not fulfill such promises. According to the Church's tradition, however, the divine services actually partake of the reality they represent. We must approach them using the gifts of faith to see God acting in our midst from within these services and calling us out of our daily existence into a new life—the starting point for the creation of a new world. Liturgical worship reminds us time after time that our God, who cannot be explained by human concepts, still lovingly calls us to be one with Him. This is a task which calls for everything that we are so that we might become even more.

The priest who serves also has the duty to offer the prayers with conviction and devotion. His own spiritual life should prepare him to preach clearly and with faith, to pray sincerely and with meaning, and to strive to make the liturgical actions express outwardly what they are truly accomplishing within the Church. It is, after all, our conviction that liturgical worship goes beyond symbols and rituals to the reality of God acting in our midst. This is why priests have often been enjoined to fast in preparation for serving the holy mysteries.

LITURGY AND COMMUNITY

Another dimension of liturgical piety is rooted in our understanding of liturgy as an action of the community. Any act of liturgical worship, no matter how small, is a gathering of the Body with Christ its Head. As such it stands as a witness against the strong trend toward individualism and privacy which diminishes the communal dimension of human life. God, however, has created and called us from all the nations and races of the earth to be one people: "Once you were no people, but now you are God's people" (1 Pt 2:10). Our Lord prayed that we be a people whose unity reflects the oneness of God: "... one, even as we [the Father and Jesus] are one" (Jn 17:11). It is in this context that St. Augustine is reputed to have said, "A solitary Christian is not a Christian." Liturgical piety acknowledges that every liturgical assembly is an affirmation and strengthening of the Church as one Body in Christ: "Where two or three are gathered in my name, there am I in their midst" (Mt 18:20).

Similarly, true liturgical piety cannot be separated from the love of our neighbor. As St Maximos the Confessor points out, the aim of the Church's mysteries is to enable each of us to become "as much as possible like Christ and bringing into open manifestation through Christ-like behavior the gift of the Holy Spirit given once by holy baptism."[54] As mutual forgiveness and reconciliation are the prerequisites for a worshipping community, care for those in need are its first consequence. Our liturgical life "results in identifying one's self as far as in one lies, as God as done, with the man who is in want of any kind of help: not letting him go uncared for and destitute, but taking the trouble to show by our deeds that our affection for both God and neighbor is alive."[55] The Divine Liturgy, the holy mysteries and the daily services are all occasions for deepening our sense of faith and our feelings toward God and others.

IN CONCLUSION

The richness and variety of the Byzantine liturgical tradition has only been hinted at in these pages. It is rare that any one community observes many of the services indicated in the typikon. Even those living in an intense monastic setting may not experience all of the rites and celebrations found in the various liturgical books. But the liturgical way of life is not based on the number and kind of services one attends, but on the degree to which the paschal mystery has become the focus of our inner life.

Technology answers many of our physical human needs, but it is incapable of responding to the needs of our inmost being, of our spirit. Mother Teresa has observed that, while Asia is materially poor, the Western world is spiritually deprived. She asks which poverty is greater. Liturgical worship confronts these deeper human needs and at the same time raises our consciousness to a new knowledge and understanding. The task is difficult in a world which entertains, challenges and stimulates our senses to a point of potentially numbing them. We obviously do not want to destroy the material quality of life that has been achieved through the genuine desire to better human life in every way. Our greater challenge lies in integrating eternal spiritual values into our everyday, material world and making it relevant to the true, the beautiful and the just. Liturgical worship responds to this fundamental human need by inviting us to "set aside all earthly cares" that would obscure the presence of God in our lives. It calls us out of our own subjectivity into community expressions of the love God has shown us by His works in our behalf. Here the Lord's teaching that "only with difficulty will a rich man enter the Kingdom of God" (Mt 19:23) takes on new meaning. The Kingdom remains open to us in communal worship, despite the difficulty of transcending our modern culture. Through our union with God, we are given new eyes and a new heart. Having received Him, we are able to sing with our whole hearts, "we have seen the true light, we have received the heavenly Spirit, we have found the true faith."

Notes

CHAPTER ONE: FAITH EXPRESSED IN WORSHIP

[1] See 1 Kings 19:11–13 (LXX, 3 Kings).

[2] "Holy God... Glory to the Father... All-holy Trinity, have mercy on us..." and the rest.

[3] In Greek, *logikyn latreia*, literally "rational worship" or "the worship offered by mind and heart" (NEB). This term is used in the Divine Liturgy of St. John Chrysostom to describe the Eucharistic oblation, both in the epiclesis and the commemorations which follow.

[4] Irenaeus, *Against Heresies*, 4.18, in Nicholas Ouspensky, *Evening Worship in the Orthodox Church*, trans. Paul Lazor (Crestwood, NY: St. Vladimir's Seminary Press, 1985), 200.

[5] cf. John Chrysostom, *Victory over Death*, 1, ed. A. Hamman in *The Paschal Mystery* (Staten Island, NY: Alba House, 1969), 98.

[6] Maximus the Confessor, *Mystagogy*, 2, trans. George C. Berthold in *Maximus Confessor, Selected Writings* (New York: Paulist Press, 1985), 188.

CHAPTER TWO: OUR SANCTIFICATION IN TIME

[7] Maximus the Confessor, *Fifth Century on Various Texts*, in *The Philokalia*, Vol. 2, trans. G. E. H. Palmer, Philip Sherrard and Kallistos Ware (London and Boston: Faber and Faber, 1981), 273.

[8] Clement, *Stromata*, 7.7, in Paul L. Bradshaw, *Daily Prayer in the Early Church* (London: Alcuin Club, SPCK, 1981), 47.

[9] Anonymous, *The Way of a Pilgrim*, trans. Helen Bacovin (Garden City, NY: Image Books, 1978), 18.

[10]For the division of the services refer to various articles by Juan Mateos, S.J., especially "Quelques problèmes de l'orthos byzantine," *Proche-Orient Chrétien (Jerusalem, 11 (1961): 17-35; 201-225;* "*L'office du soir,*" *in* Revue du clergé Africain (January 1964): 3-25; "La Synaxe monastique des Vêspres byzantines," *Orientalia Christiana Periodica,* 36 (Rome, 1970): 248-272. A highly recommended article on Vespers is Robert Taft, S.J., "Thanksgiving for the Light. Toward a Theology of Vespers," *Diakonia* (New York, John XXIII Center, Fordham University) 13 (1978): 27-50; revised in *Beyond East and West* (Washington, DC: The Pastoral Press, 1984), 127-150.

[11]Eusebius of Caesaria, *Commentary on Ps 64*, PG 23, 640, quoted in Taft, op. cit., 132.

[12]*De Castigatione*, 46.309 in C. S. Mosna, *Storia della Domenica dalle Origini fino agli Inizi del V Secolo* (Rome: Libreria Editrice dell'Università Gregoriana, 1969), 354.

CHAPTER THREE: THE YEARLY CYCLE

[13] It is worth noting that the first translations of the Greek liturgical texts into Slavonic chose not to translate this word, but to simply transliterate it. This same development may today be found in English.

[14]Adolf Adam, *The Liturgical Year* (New York: Pueblo Publishing Co., 1981), 84.

[15]Ibid., 88.

[16] cf. Rene-Georges Coquin, "Les Origines de l'Epiphanie en Egypte," *Noel-Epiphanie: Retour du Christ* (Paris: Lex Orandi, 1967), 40

[17] Our English word "lent" comes from the Old-English "lengthen" which was used for spring, since at this time of year in the northern hemisphere the days lengthen. The Triodion speaks of this period as the "springtime of the soul".

[18] Adam, op. cit., 144-145.

[19] Cf. Hippolytus of Rome, *The Commentary on Daniel*, IV, 23.

[20] Egeria, *Diary of a Pilgrimage*, trans. George E. Gingras (New York: Ancient Christian Writers, Newman Press, 1970), 126-127.

[21] On the third Sunday of Great Lent, the Cross is likewise venerated by bringing it to the middle of the Church for reverence by the faithful.

[22] 1 Clement 5:4-7, trans. C. C. Richardson in *Library of Christian Classics: Alexandrian Christianity* (London, Philadelphia, 1954), 46.

[23] In contrast to the conception of Christ, the perfect man (celebrated exactly nine months before Christmas), the conceptions of the Theotokos and St John the Baptist are observed one day short of nine months in the Byzantine calendar. The Ruthenian and Ukrainian metropolias in the United States have transferred this feast to December 8 to coincide with the Roman feast of the Immaculate Conception.

[24] *Protoevangelion of James*, in Edgar Hennecke and Wilhelm Schneemelcher, *New Testament Apocrypha, Vol. 1* (Philadelphia: The Westminster Press, 1959), 374-388.

[25] An English version of the Paraklisis may be found in *Byzantine Daily Worship*, ed. Most Rev. Joseph Raya and Baron Jose de Vinck (Allendale, NJ: Alleluia Press, 1969), 927–955.

[26] A translation of the Akathistos Hymn to the Mother of God may be found in ibid., 957–980.

CHAPTER FOUR: THE DIVINE LITURGY, THE FULFILLMENT OF TIME

[27] Literally, "the Savior's command" (*tis sotiriou*)

[28] *Homily on the Letter to the Hebrews* 17.6.

[29] *Homily on the Gospel of St Matthew* 82.5.

[30] *On the Orthodox Faith* 13.

[31] Louis Bouyer, *Eucharist* (South Bend, IN: Notre Dame Press, 1968), 102.

[32] *Homily 50 on Pentecost.*

[33] This translation is the one used by the Metropolitan Province of Pittsburgh (Pittsburgh, PA: Byzantine Seminary Press, 1965). Others may translate "purification," as "vigilance" or "sobriety of soul."

[34] For further information on the paragraph, read Bouyer, op. cit., 281–314.

[35] Ibid., 268.

[36] Most Byzantine Churches reserve both the presanctified Body and Blood of Christ, by intincting the consecrated bread with the precious Blood. The Ruthenian Church reserves only the Body of our Lord, which appears to be the more ancient custom: Nicholas Ouspensky, *Evening Worship in the Orthodox Church*, trans. Paul Lazor (Crestwood, NY: St. Vladimir's Seminary Press, 1985), 149–151; 208–220. This may stem from the belief that the union of the consecrated Body of our Lord with the unconsecrated wine sanctified this wine by contact.

[37] Some Greek parishes still maintain this ancient custom.

CHAPTER FIVE: THE HOLY MYSTERIES, SANCTIFICATION OF LIFE

[38] Homily 1 on 1 Corinthians, 7.

[39] *Constitution on the Church*, 1.

[40] Georg Wagner, "Bussdisziplin in der Tradition des Ostens," (The Discipline of Penance in the Eastern Tradition) in *Liturgie et Rémission des Peschés* (Rome: Edizioni Liturgiche, 1975), 254.

[41] Elie Mélia, "The Sacrament of Anointing of the Sick: Its Historical Development and Current Practice," in *Temple of the Holy Spirit*, trans. Matthew J. O'Connell (New York: Pueblo Publishing Co., 1983), 151–157.

[42] Simeon of Thessalonica, *Dialogue*, cited in Paul Evdokimov, *La Pensee Orthodoxe*, He concludes, "In the ancient practice, each mystery was arranged as a component of the eucharistic liturgy, which impressed upon the bestower and the recipient a kind of definite seal." Thus, even when baptisms or marriages are celebrated apart from the Sunday Liturgy, they are concluded with the "eighth day" prayers at the next Sunday Liturgy.

[43] Prayer for blessing the oil in the rite of baptism.

[44] *Mystagogical Catechesis* 3.1. An "antitype" is a term given in patristic thought to the mysteries as making present that which they represent. Thus baptism is a type of the death and resurrection of Christ and the holy gifts are a type of the body and blood of Christ.

[45] The translation in *The Divine Liturgy of Our Father St. John Chrysostom* (Pittsburgh, PA: 1965), 44, "...so that we may live according to Your truth," is not literal and differs from the original Greek.

[46] *Life of Moses*, 10.

[47] "Rite of Penance," in *The Rites of the Catholic Church*, (New York: Pueblo Publishing Co., 1976), 342.

[48] cf. *Constitution on the Church, 29; Decree on the Catholic Eastern Churches*, 17.

[49] *Constitution on the Liturgy*, 73.

[50] Pseudo-Dionysius the Areopagite, *The Ecclesiastical Hierarchy* VI

[51]Pseudo-Dionysius the Areopagite, *The Ecclesiastical Hierarchy* VII

[52] Sticheron to the Holy Spirit ("O heavenly King...").

CHAPTER SIX: LIVING LITURGICALLY

[53] *The Great Catechism*, 40.

[54] Maximos the Confessor, *Mystagogia* 24.

[55] ibid.

Glossary of Liturgical and Theological Terms

ANAPHORA — The Great Eucharistic Prayer, the heart of the Divine Liturgy, beginning with the invocation, "Let us give thanks to the Lord," and concluding with the prayers of intercession.

APOSTICHA STICHERA — Stichera interpolated between certain stichi (psalm verses) sung at the end of matins and vespers.

BEGINNING PRAYERS — The set of prayers found at the beginning of most Byzantine liturgical services and personal devotions. The are: Holy God... (three times), Glory... Now... All-holy Trinity... Lord, haver mercy (three times), Glory... Now..., Our Father....

CANON — A poetical composition of nine odes, each made up of several troparia, which is sung at matins and certain other services. The theme of each ode is taken from a corresponding biblical canticle.

CHERUBIKON — The hymn sung at the great entrance in the Divine Liturgy most days of the year. It takes its name from the first words of the hymn, "Let us, who mystically represent the cherubim, ..."

DOXOLOGY — The hymn "Glory to God in the highest" to which is added certain verses from the Hymn of St Ambrose (the "Te Deum"). One version (the Lesser Doxology) is recited at daily matins and compline; a more solemn form (the Great Doxology) is sung at matins on Sundays and feasts.

GENTILE — The Jewish sense that they were an elect or chosen people caused them to separate themselves from the non-Jews or Gentiles who were not so chosen. The first Christians were originally drawn from the Jews. Later Gentiles were also converted to Christ.

GREAT ENTRANCE — At the Divine Liturgy, the transfer of the holy gifts from the table of preparation to the Holy Table. It is preceeded by the little entrance, during which the Gospel Book is brought forth.

GREAT FAST — The 40-day fast period preceeding Great Week and the Paschal celebration. It is called "great" to distinguish it from the less austere and shorter fasts before the feasts of Christmas, Ss. Peter and Paul, and the Dormition of the Theotokos.

GREAT (AND HOLY) WEEK — The week preceeding Pascha, each day of which commemorates one or more events of the death and resurrection of Christ.

GREAT SYNAPTE — The opening litany at vespers, matins, and the Divine Liturgy, beginning with the words "In peace let us pray to the Lord."

HOLY DOORS — The central doors of the icon screen on which are depicted icons of the annunciation and/or the four evangelists. They are usually closed except for the principal parts of vespers, matins, and the Divine Liturgy. Along with the other doors of the screen, they remain open throughout the week of Pascha (Bright Week) in rememberance of the opened tomb.

(HOLY) MYSTERIES — The Eastern term for sacraments, referring to the hidden power of God working in them.

PRESANCTIFIED LITURGY — A combination of Great Vespers and a Communion Service, patterned on the Divine Liturgy, served during the Great Fast.

RESURRECTION GOSPELS — Eleven pericopes from the four Gospels concerning the appearances of the risen Christ which are read at matins on successive Sundays during the year.

SEVENTH ECUMENICAL COUNCIL — The Second Council of Nicaea (787) which proclaimed the validity and necessity of icons as a consequence of the incarnation of Christ.

STICHERON (PL. STICHERA) — A Byzantine liturgical chant, usually longer than a troparion, found in vespers, matins, and certain other services.

THEOTOKOS — The title "God-bearer", accorded to the Virgin Mary at the Council of Ephesus (431) as a legitimate expression of her role in the incarnation of Christ.

TYPICON — The rule or arrangment of prayers, hymns, and readings in the various services of the Byzantine tradition. The "Great Typicon" or "Typikon of the Great Church" is the order followed at Constantinople.

TRISAGION PRAYERS — See **BEGINNING PRAYERS**.

TROPARION — A brief liturgical chant, usually referring to the theme of the feast celebrated.

VIGIL DIVINE LITURGY — A service combining the beginning of Great Vespers and the Eucharistic Liturgy served on the eves of certain feasts or on feasts which are also fast days.

Index of Scripture References and Citations

Old Testament

New Testament

Index of Patristic Citations